A DAY IN JUNE. (See p. 230.)

EIGHT-BOOK SERIES

BROOKS'S READERS

EIGHTH YEAR

BY

STRATTON D. BROOKS

SUPERINTENDENT OF SCHOOLS, BOSTON, MASSACHUSETTS

NEW YORK ∴ CINCINNATI ∴ CHICAGO
AMERICAN BOOK COMPANY

Copyright, 1906, by
AMERICAN BOOK COMPANY
Copyright, 1907, Tokyo.

BROOKS'S READERS.   EIGHTH YEAR.
E-P 5

CONTENTS

		PAGE
Books	John Ruskin	9
My Brute Neighbors	Henry D. Thoreau	14
September Days	George Arnold	21
Autumn's Mirth	Samuel Minturn Peck	22
Under the Greenwood Tree	William Shakespeare	23
The High Court of Inquiry	J. G. Holland	24
Moses goes to the Fair	Oliver Goldsmith	31
A Legend of Bregenz	Adelaide Procter	36
Parables	Benjamin Franklin	43
Nobility	Alice Cary	47
Tact and Talent	From "London Atlas"	48
The Man without a Country	Edward Everett Hale	51
The Battle of Lexington	George Bancroft	63
Lexington	Oliver Wendell Holmes	67
The Bell of Liberty	J. T. Headley	69
The Rising in 1776	T. Buchanan Read	73
Raleigh and Queen Elizabeth	Sir Walter Scott	77
Silas Marner and Eppie	George Eliot	83
The Bell of Atri	H. W. Longfellow	93
The Mocking Bird	Alexander Wilson	98
The Water Ouzel	John Muir	102
The Daffodils	William Wordsworth	107
Where lies the Land?	Arthur Hugh Clough	108
The Czar and the Angel	"Cossack Fairy Tales"	109
The Sea Voyage	Charles Lamb	120

		PAGE
The Lesson of the Fern	Mary L. Bolles Branch	127
Oliver Goldsmith	William M. Thackeray	129
The Village of Auburn	Oliver Goldsmith	131
The Village Preacher	Oliver Goldsmith	132
The Village Schoolmaster	Oliver Goldsmith	135
A Great Philosopher	Charles Morris	136
The Story of Lafayette	Alma Holman Burton	141
The American Flag	J. Rodman Drake	153
Liberty and Union	Daniel Webster	154
Patriotism	George William Curtis	156
What makes a Nation?	W. D. Nesbit	158
The Cheerful Locksmith	Charles Dickens	159
The Lost Child. An Australian Story	Henry Kingsley	161
Hervé Riel	Robert Browning	170
The Story of my Boyhood	Hans Christian Andersen	177
Douglas and Marmion	Sir Walter Scott	186
The Battle of Blenheim	Robert Southey	189
Burial of Sir John Moore	Charles Wolfe	192
Among the Icebergs	Walter A. Wyckoff	193
Passing the Icebergs	T. Buchanan Read	201
Rip Van Winkle	Washington Irving	204
The Bells	Edgar Allan Poe	210
Little Gavroche	Victor Hugo	213
Oration of Mark Antony	William Shakespeare	225
A Day in June	James Russell Lowell	230
Speech and Silence	Thomas Carlyle	233
Opportunity	Edward Rowland Sill	235
The Mystery of Life	John Ruskin	236
Over the Hill	George Macdonald	239
The Sun is Down	Joanna Baillie	240
Finale	William M. Thackeray	240
APPENDIX		241

ACKNOWLEDGMENTS

THE selections from Henry Wadsworth Longfellow, Henry D. Thoreau, Oliver Wendell Holmes, Alice Cary, and James Russell Lowell are used by permission of, and special arrangement with, Houghton, Mifflin & Co., the authorized publishers of the works of those authors.

Acknowledgments for the use of copyright matter are also extended to publishers and authors as follows: To Charles Scribner's Sons, for the selection from J. G. Holland's "Arthur Bonnicastle"; to John Muir, for the extract from his work on "The Mountains of California"; to Walter A. Wyckoff, for the selection entitled "Among the Icebergs"; to Samuel Minturn Peck, for his poem "Autumn's Mirth"; and to Alma Holman Burton for the adaptation of her "Story of Lafayette."

Acknowledgments are also due to Mr. W. J. Button of Chicago for valuable assistance rendered in connection with the preparation of this volume.

A LOVER OF BOOKS.

BOOKS

ALL books may be divided into two classes, — books of the hour, and books of all time. Yet it is not merely the bad book that does not last, and the good one that does. There are good books for the hour and good ones for all time; bad books for the hour and bad ones for all time. I must define the two kinds before I go on.

The good book of the hour, then, — I do not speak of the bad ones, — is simply the useful or pleasant talk of some person printed for you. Very useful often, telling you what you need to know; very pleasant often, as sensible friends' present talk would be. These bright accounts of travels, good-humored and witty discussions of question, lively or pathetic story-telling in the form of novel, firm fact-telling — all these books of the hour are the peculiar possession of the present age. We ought to be entirely thankful for them, and entirely ashamed of ourselves if we make no good use of them. But we make the worst possible use, if we allow them to usurp the place of true books; for, strictly speaking, they are not books at all, but merely letters or newspapers in good print.

Our friend's letter may be delightful, or necessary, to-day; whether worth keeping or not, is to be considered. The newspaper may be entirely proper at breakfast time, but it is not reading for all day. So, though bound up in a volume, the long letter which gives you so pleasant an account of the inns and roads and weather last year at such a place, or which tells you that amusing story, or relates such and such circumstances of interest, may not be, in the real sense of the word, a "book" at all, nor, in the real sense, to be "read."

A book is not a talked thing, but a written thing. The book of talk is printed only because its author cannot speak to thousands of people at once; if he could, he would — the volume is mere multiplication of the voice. You cannot talk to your friend in India; if you could, you would; you write instead: that is merely a way of carrying the voice. But a book is written, not to multiply the voice merely, not to carry it merely, but to preserve it. The author has something to say which he perceives to be true and useful, or helpfully beautiful. So far as he knows, no one has yet said it; so far as he knows, no one can say it. He is bound to say it, clearly and in a melodious manner if he may; clearly, at all events.

In the sum of his life he finds this to be the thing, or group of things, manifest to him; this the piece of true knowledge, or sight, which his share of sunshine and earth has allowed him to seize. He would set it down forever; carve it on a rock, if he could, saying, " This is the best of me; for the rest, I ate and drank and slept, loved and hated, like another; my life was as the vapor, and is not; but this I saw and knew: this, if anything of mine, is worth your memory." That is his " writing "; that is a " book."

Now books of this kind have been written in all ages by their greatest men — by great leaders, great statesmen, great thinkers. These are all at your choice; and life is short. You have heard as much before; yet have you measured and mapped out this short life and its possibilities? Do you know, if you read this, that you cannot read that — that what you lose to-day you cannot gain to-morrow?

Will you go and gossip with the housemaid, or the stable boy, when you may talk with queens and kings? Do you ask to be the companion of nobles? Make yourself noble, and you shall be. Do you long for the conversation of the wise? Learn to understand it and you shall hear it. But on other terms? — no. If you will not rise to them, they cannot stoop to you.

Very ready we are to say of a book, " How good this is — that is just what I think!" But the right feeling is, " How strange that is! I never thought

of that before, and yet I see it is true ; or if I do not
now, I hope I shall some day." But whether you
feel thus or not, at least be sure that you go to the
author to get at *his* meaning, not to find yours. And
be sure also, if the author is worth anything, that
you will not get at his meaning all at once; nay,
that at his whole meaning you may not for a long
time arrive in any wise. Not that he does not say
what he means, and in strong words too; but he
cannot say it all, and, what is more strange, will not,
but in a hidden way in order that he may be sure you
want it.

When, therefore, you come to a good book, you
must ask yourself, "Am I ready to work as an
Australian miner would? Are my pickaxes in good
order, and am I in good trim myself, my sleeves well
up to the elbow, and my breath good, and my
temper?" For your pickaxes are your own care,
wit, and learning; your smelting furnace is your
own thoughtful soul. Do not hope to get at any
good author's meaning without these tools and that
fire; often you will need sharpest, finest carving,
and the most careful melting, before you can gather
one grain of the precious gold. . . .

I cannot, of course, tell you what to choose for
your library, for every several mind needs different
books; but there are some books which we all need,

and which if you read as much as you ought, you will not need to have your shelves enlarged to right and left for purposes of study.

If you want to understand any subject whatever, read the best book upon it you can hear of.

A common book will often give you amusement, but it is only a noble book which will give you dear friends. . . .

Avoid that class of literature which has a knowing tone; it is the most poisonous of all.

Every good book, or piece of book, is full of admiration and awe; and it always leads you to reverence or love something with your whole heart.

It may become necessary for you, as you advance in life, to set your hand to things that need to be altered in the world; but for a young person the safest temper is one of reverence, and the safest place one of obscurity.

Certainly at present, and perhaps through all your life, your teachers are wisest when they make you content in quiet virtue; and that literature and art are best for you which point out in common life and familiar things the objects for hopeful labor and for humble love.

— JOHN RUSKIN.

MY BRUTE NEIGHBORS

THE mice which haunted my house were not the common ones, which are said to have been introduced into the country, but a wild native kind not found in the village. When I was building, one of these had its nest underneath the house, and before I had laid the second floor and swept out the shavings, would come out regularly at lunch time and pick up the crumbs at my feet. It probably had never seen a man before; and it soon became quite familiar and would run over my shoes and up my clothes. It could readily ascend the sides of the room by short impulses, like the squirrel, which it resembled in its motions.

At length, as I leaned with my elbow on the bench one day, it ran up my clothes and along my sleeve and round and round the paper which held my dinner, while I kept the latter closed, and dodged and played at bopeep with it; and when at last I held still a piece of cheese between my thumb and finger, it came and nibbled it, sitting in my hand, and afterwards cleaned its face and paws, like a fly, and walked away.

A phœbe soon built in my shed, and a robin for protection in a pine which grew against the house. In June the partridge, which is so shy a bird, led her brood past my windows, from the woods in the rear to the front of my house, clucking and calling to them like a hen, and in all her behavior proving herself the hen of the woods. The young suddenly disperse on your approach, at a signal from the mother, as if a whirlwind had swept them away, and they so exactly resemble the dried leaves and twigs, that many a traveler has placed his foot in the midst of a brood and heard the whir of the old bird as she flew off and  her anxious calls and mewing, or seen her trail her wings to attract his attention, without suspecting their neighborhood.

The parent will sometimes roll and spin around before you in such a deshabille that you cannot, for a few moments, detect what kind of creature it is. The young squat still and flat, often running their heads under a leaf, and mind only their mother's directions given from a distance, nor will your approach make them run again and betray themselves. You may even tread on them, or have your eyes on them for a minute, without discovering them. I have held them in my open hand at such a time, and still their only care, obedient to their mother and their instinct, was to squat there without fear or trembling.

So perfect is this instinct, that once, when I laid them on the leaves again, and one accidentally fell on its side, it was found with the rest in exactly the same position ten minutes afterwards. They are not callow like the young of most birds, but more perfectly developed and precocious even than chickens. The remarkably adult yet innocent expression of their open and serene eyes is very memorable. All intelligence seems reflected in them. They suggest not merely the purity of infancy, but a wisdom clarified by experience. Such an eye was not born when the bird was, but is coeval with the sky it reflects. The woods do not yield another such a gem. The traveler does not often look into such a limpid well.

The ignorant or reckless sportsman often shoots the parent at such a time, and leaves these innocents to fall a prey to some prowling beast or bird, or gradually mingle with the decaying leaves which they so much resemble. It is said that when hatched by a hen they will directly disperse on some alarm, and so are lost, for they never hear the mother's call which gathers them again. These were my hens and chickens.

It is remarkable how many creatures live wild and free though secret in the woods and still sustain themselves in the neighborhood of towns, suspected by hunters only. How retired the otter manages to live here! He grows to be four feet long, as big as a small boy, perhaps without any human being getting a glimpse of him. I formerly saw the raccoon in the woods behind where my house is built, and probably still hear their whinnering at night.

Commonly I rested an hour or two in the shade at noon, after planting, and ate my lunch and read a little by a spring, which was the source of a swamp and of a brook. The approach to this was through a succession of descending grassy hollows, full of young pitch pines, into a larger wood about the swamp. There, in a very secluded and shaded spot, under a spreading white pine, was yet a clean, firm sward to sit on. I had dug out the spring and made a well of clear, gray water, where I could dip up a pailful without roiling it, and thither I went for this purpose almost every day in midsummer, when the pond was warmest.

Thither, too, the woodcock led her brood, to probe the mud for worms, flying but a foot above them down the bank, while they ran in a troop beneath; but at last, spying me, she would leave her young and circle round and round me, nearer and nearer, till within four or five feet, pretending broken wings and legs, to attract my attention and get off her young, who would have already taken up their march, with faint, wiry peep, single file through the swamp as she directed. Or I heard the peep of the young when I could not see the parent bird.

There, too, the turtle doves sat over the spring, or fluttered from bough to bough of the soft white pines over my head; or the red squirrel, coursing down the nearest bough, was particularly familiar and inquisitive. You only need sit still long enough in some attractive spot in the woods, that all its inhabitants may exhibit themselves to you by turns.

I was witness to events of a less peaceful character. One day when I went out to my woodpile, or rather my pile of stumps, I observed two large ants, the one red, and the other much larger, nearly half an inch long, and black, fiercely contending with each other. Having once got hold, they never let go, but struggled and wrestled and rolled on the chips incessantly. Looking farther, I was surprised to find that the chips were covered with such combatants; that it was not a *duellum*, but a *bellum*, — a war between two races of ants, the red always pitted against the black, and frequently two red ones to one black. The legions of these Myrmidons covered all the hills and vales in my woodyard, and the ground was already strewn with the dead and the dying, both red and black.

I watched a couple that were fast locked in each other's embraces, in a little sunny valley amid the chips, now at noonday prepared to fight till the sun went down, or life went out. The smaller red champion had fastened himself like a vise to his adversary's front, and through all the tumbling on that field never for an instant ceased to gnaw at one of his feelers near the root, having already caused the other to go by the board; while the stronger black one dashed him from side to side, and, as I saw on looking nearer, had already divested him of several of his members. They fought with more pertinacity than bulldogs. Neither manifested the least disposition to retreat. It was evident that their battle cry was "Conquer or die."

In the meanwhile there came along a single red ant on the hillside of this valley, evidently full of excitement, who either had dispatched his foe, or had not yet taken part in the battle — probably the latter, for he had lost none of his limbs — whose mother had charged him to return *with* his shield or *upon* it. Or, perchance, he was some Achilles, who had nourished his wrath apart, and had now come to avenge or rescue his Patroclus.

He saw this unequal combat afar — for the blacks were nearly twice the size of the reds — he drew near with rapid pace till he stood on his guard within half an inch of the combatants; then, watching his opportunity, he sprang upon the black warrior and commenced his operations near the root of his right fore leg, leaving the foe to select among his own members; and so there were three united for life, as if a new kind of attraction had been invented which put all other locks and cements to shame.

Certainly there is not the fight recorded in Concord history at least, if in the history of America, that will bear a moment's comparison with this, whether for the numbers engaged in it, or for the patriotism and heroism displayed. I never learned which party was victorious, nor the cause of the war; but I felt for the rest of that day as if I had had my feelings excited and harrowed by witnessing the struggle, the ferocity and carnage, of a human battle before my door.

— HENRY D. THOREAU.

From " Walden."

SEPTEMBER DAYS

In flickering light and shade the broad stream goes,
  With cool, dark nooks and checkered, rippling shallows;
Through reedy fens its sluggish current flows,
  Where lilies grow and purple-blossomed mallows.

The aster blooms above its eddies shine,
  With pollened bees about them humming slowly,
And in the meadow lands the drowsy kine
  Make music with their sweet bells, tinkling lowly.

The shrill cicala, on the hillside tree,
  Sounds to its mate a note of love or warning;
And turtle doves reëcho, plaintively,
  From upland fields, a soft, melodious mourning.

A golden haze conceals the horizon,
  A golden sunshine slants across the meadows;
The pride and prime of summer time is gone,
  But beauty lingers in these autumn shadows.

O sweet September! thy first breezes bring
  The dry leaf's rustle and the squirrel's laughter,
The cool, fresh air, whence health and vigor spring,
  And promise of exceeding joy hereafter.

— George Arnold.

AUTUMN'S MIRTH

'Tis all a myth that autumn grieves,
For, watch the rain among the leaves;
With silver fingers dimly seen,
It makes each leaf a tambourine,
And swings and leaps with elfin mirth
To kiss the brow of mother earth;
Or, laughing 'mid the trembling grass,
It nods a greeting as you pass.
Oh! hear the rain amid the leaves,
'Tis all a myth that autumn grieves!

'Tis all a myth that autumn grieves,
For, list the wind among the sheaves;
Far sweeter than the breath of May,
Or storied scents of old Cathay,
It blends the perfumes rare and good
Of spicy pine and hickory wood,
And with a voice in gayest chime,
It prates of rifled mint and thyme.
Oh! scent the wind among the sheaves,
'Tis all a myth that autumn grieves!

'Tis all a myth that autumn grieves,
Behold the wondrous web she weaves!
By viewless hands her thread is spun
Of evening vapors shyly won.

Across the grass, from side to side,
A myriad unseen shuttles glide
Throughout the night, till on the height
Aurora leads the laggard light.
Behold the wondrous web she weaves,
'Tis all a myth that autumn grieves!
— SAMUEL MINTURN PECK

UNDER THE GREENWOOD TREE

UNDER the greenwood tree,
Who loves to lie with me,
And tune his merry note
Unto the sweet bird's throat,
Come hither, come hither, come hither!
Here shall he see
No enemy
But winter and rough weather.

Who doth ambition shun,
And loves to live i' the sun,
Seeking the food he eats,
And pleased with what he gets,
Come hither, come hither, come hither!
Here shall he see
No enemy
But winter and rough weather.
— WILLIAM SHAKESPEARE.

THE HIGH COURT OF INQUIRY

It must have been three weeks or a month after I entered the school that, on a rainy holiday, I was met by two boys who ordered me peremptorily to "halt." Both had staves in their hands, taller than themselves, and one of them addressed me with the words: "Arthur Bonnicastle, you are arrested in the name of the High Court of Inquiry, and ordered to appear before that august tribunal, to answer for your sins and misdemeanors. Right about face!"

The movement had so much the air of mystery and romance that I was about equally pleased and scared. Marching between the two officials, I was led directly to my own room, which I was surprised to find quite full of boys, all of whom were grave and silent.

"We have secured the offender," said one of my captors, "and now have the satisfaction of presenting him before this honorable society."

"The prisoner will stand in the middle of the room and look at me," said the presiding officer, in a tone of dignified severity.

I was accordingly marched into the middle of the room and left alone, where I stood with folded arms, as became the grand occasion.

"Arthur Bonnicastle," said the officer before mentioned, "you are brought before the High Court of Inquiry on a charge of telling so many lies that no dependence whatever can be placed upon your words. What have you to reply to this charge? Are you guilty or not guilty?"

"I am not guilty. Who says I am?" I exclaimed indignantly.

"Henry Hulm, advance!" said the officer.

Henry rose, and walking by me, took a position near the officer at the head of the room.

"Henry Hulm, you will look upon the prisoner and tell the Court whether you know him."

"I know him well. He is my chum," replied Henry.

"What is his character?"

"He is bright and very amiable."

"Do you consider him a boy of truth and veracity?"

"I do not."

"Has he deceived you?" inquired the officer. "If he has, please to state the occasion and circumstances."

"No, your Honor. He has never deceived me. I always know whether he is speaking the truth or not."

"Have you ever told him of his crimes, and warned him to desist from them?"

"I have," replied Henry, "many times."

"Has he shown any disposition to mend?"

"None at all, your Honor."

"What is the character of his falsehood?"

"He tells," replied Henry, "stunning stories about himself. Great things are always happening to him, and he is always performing wonderful deeds."

I now began, with great shame and confusion, to realize that I was exposed to ridicule. The tears came into my eyes and dropped from my cheeks, but I would not yield to the impulse either to cry or to attempt to fly.

"Will you give us some specimens of his stories?" said the officer.

"I will," responded Henry, "but I can do it best by asking him some questions."

"Very well," said the officer, with a polite bow. "Pursue the course you think best."

"Arthur," said Henry, addressing me directly, "did you ever tell me that, when you and your father were on the way to this school, your horse went so fast that he ran down a black fox in the middle of the road, and cut off his tail with the wheel of the chaise, and that you sent that tail to one of your sisters to wear in her winter hat?"

"Yes, I did," I responded with my face flaming and painful with shame.

"And did your said horse really run down said fox in the middle of said road, and cut off said tail; and did you send home said tail to said sister to be worn in said hat?" inquired the judge, with a low gruff voice. "The prisoner will answer so that all can hear."

"No," I replied, and, looking for some justification of my story, I added: "But I did see a black fox, — a real black fox, as plain as day!"

"Oh! oh! oh!" ran around the room in chorus. "He did see a black fox, a real black fox, as plain as day!"

"The witness will pursue his inquiries," said the officer.

"Arthur," Henry continued, " did you or did you not tell me that when on the way to this school you overtook Mr. and Mrs. Bird in their wagon, that you were invited into the wagon by Mrs. Bird, and that one of Mr. Bird's horses chased a calf on the road, caught it by the ear and tossed it over the fence, and broke its leg?"

"I s'pose I did," I said, growing desperate.

"And did said horse really chase said calf, and catch him by said ear, and toss him over said fence, and break said leg?" inquired the officer.

"He didn't catch him by the ear," I replied doggedly, "but he really did chase a calf."

"Oh! oh! oh!" chimed in the chorus. "He didn't catch him by the ear, but he really did chase a calf!"

"Witness," said the officer, "you will pursue your inquiries." . . .

"Did you or did you not," said Henry, turning to me again, "tell me that one day, when dining at your aunt's, you saw a magic portrait of a boy upon the wall, that came and went, and came and went like a shadow or a ghost?"

As Henry asked this question he stood between two windows, while the lower portion of his person was hidden by a table behind which he had retired.

His face was lighted by a half smile, and I saw him literally in a frame, as I had first seen the picture to which he had alluded. In a moment I became oblivious to everything around me except Henry's face. The portrait was there again before my eyes. Every lineament and even the peculiar pose of the head were recalled to me.

"Did you or did you not tell me the story about the portrait, Arthur?"

"Yes," I responded, "and it looked just like you. Oh! it did, it did, it did! There — turn your head a little more that way — so! It was a perfect picture of you, Henry. You never could imagine such a likeness."

"You are a little blower, you are," volunteered Jack Linton, from a corner.

"Order! order! order!"

Looking around upon the boys, and realizing what had been done and what was in progress, I went into a fit of hearty crying, that distressed them quite as much as my previous mood had done. At this moment a strange silence seized the assembly. All eyes were directed toward the door upon which my back was turned. I wheeled around to find the cause of the interruption. There, in the doorway, towering above us all, and looking questioningly down upon the little assembly, stood Mr. Bird.

"What does this mean?" inquired the master.

I flew to his side and took his hand. The officer who had presided explained that they had been trying to break Arthur Bonnicastle of lying and they were about to order him to report to the master for confession and correction.

Then Mr. Bird took a chair and patiently heard the whole story. Without a reproach further than saying that he thought me much too young for experiments of the kind they had instituted in the case, he explained to them and to me the nature of my misdemeanors.

"The boy has a great deal of imagination," he said, "and a strong love of approbation. Somebody has flattered his power of invention, probably, and to secure admiration he has exercised it until he has acquired the habit of exaggeration. I am glad if he has learned, even by the severe means which have been used, that if he wishes to be loved and admired he must always tell the exact truth, neither more nor less. If you had come to me, I could have told you all about the lad, and instituted a better mode of dealing with him. But I venture to say that he is cured. Aren't you, Arthur?" And he stooped and lifted me to his face and locked into my eyes.

"I don't think I shall do it any more," I said.

Bidding the boys disperse, he carried me downstairs into his own room, and charged me with kindly counsel. I went out from the interview humbled and without a revengeful thought in my heart toward the boys who had brought me to my trial. I saw that they were my friends, and I was determined to prove myself worthy of their friendship.

— J. G. HOLLAND.

From " Arthur Bonnicastle," published by Charles Scribner's Sons.

MOSES GOES TO THE FAIR

As we were now to hold up our heads a little higher in the world, my wife suggested that it would be proper to sell the colt, which was grown old, at a neighboring fair, and buy us a horse that would carry single or double upon an occasion, and make a pretty appearance at church or upon a visit. This at first I opposed stoutly; but it was as stoutly defended. However, as I weakened, my antagonist gained strength, till at last we agreed to part with him.

As the fair happened on the following day, I had intentions of going myself; but my wife persuaded me that I had got a cold, and nothing could prevail upon her to permit me from home. "No, my dear," said she, " our son Moses is a discreet boy, and can buy and sell to very good advantage. You know all our great bargains are of his purchasing. He always stands out and higgles, and actually tires them till he gets a bargain."

As I had some opinion of my son's prudence, I was willing enough to intrust him with this commission; and the next morning I perceived his sisters mighty busy in fitting out Moses for the fair; trimming his hair, brushing his buckles, and cocking his hat with pins. The business of the toilet being over, we had at last the satisfaction of seeing him mounted upon the colt, with a deal box before him to bring home groceries in.

He had on a coat made of that cloth they call thunder and lightning, which, though grown too short, was much too good to be thrown away. His waistcoat was of gosling-green, and his sisters had tied his hair with a broad black ribbon. We all followed him several paces from the door, bawling after him, "Good luck! good luck!" till we could see him no longer. . . .

As it was now almost nightfall, I began to wonder what could keep our son so long at the fair. "Never mind our son," cried my wife; "depend upon it, he knows what he is about. I'll warrant we'll never see him sell his hen on a rainy day. I have seen him buy such bargains as would amaze one. I'll tell you a good story about that, that will make you split your sides with laughing — But as I live, yonder comes Moses without a horse, and the box at his back."

As she spoke, Moses came slowly on foot, and sweating under the deal box, which he had strapped round his shoulders like a peddler.

"Welcome, welcome, Moses! Well, my boy, what have you brought us from the fair?"

"I have brought you myself," said Moses, with a sly look, and resting the box on the dresser.

"Ay, Moses," cried my wife, "that we know; but where is the horse?"

"I have sold him," replied Moses, "for three pounds five shillings and twopence."

"Well done, my good boy," returned she; "I knew you would touch them off. Between ourselves, three pounds five shillings and twopence is no bad day's work. Come, let us have it then."

"I have brought back no money," cried Moses again: "I have laid it all out in a bargain, — and here it is," pulling out a bundle from his breast: "here they are, — a gross of green spectacles, with silver rims and shagreen cases."

"A gross of green spectacles!" repeated my wife, in a faint voice. "And you have parted with the colt, and brought us back nothing but a gross of green paltry spectacles!"

"Dear mother," cried the boy, "why won't you
VIII. — 3

listen to reason? I had them a dead bargain, or I should not have bought them. The silver rims alone will sell for double the money."

"A fig for the silver rims!" cried my wife in a passion: "I dare swear they won't sell for above half the money at the rate of broken silver, five shillings an ounce."

"You need be under no uneasiness," said I, "about selling the rims, for they are not worth sixpence; for I perceive they are only copper varnished over."

"What!" cried my wife; "not silver! the rims not silver!"

"No," cried I; "no more silver than your saucepan."

"And so," returned she, "we have parted with the colt, and have only got a gross of green spectacles, with copper rims and shagreen cases? A murrain take such trumpery! The blockhead has been imposed upon, and should have known his company better."

"There, my dear," cried I, "you are wrong; he should not have known them at all."

"To bring me such stuff!" returned she; "if I had them, I would throw them into the fire."

"There again you are wrong, my dear," said I; "for though they are copper, we will keep them by us, as copper spectacles, you know, are better than nothing."

By this time the unfortunate Moses was undeceived. He now saw that he had been imposed upon by a prowling sharper, who, observing his figure, had marked him for an easy prey. I therefore asked the circumstances of his deception. He sold the horse, it seems, and walked the fair in search of another. A reverend-looking man brought him to a tent, under pretense of having one to sell.

"Here," continued Moses, "we met another man, very well dressed, who desired to borrow twenty pounds upon these, saying that he wanted money, and would dispose of them for a third of the value.

The first gentleman whispered me to buy them, and cautioned me not to let so good an offer pass. I sent to Mr. Flamborough, and they talked him up as finely as they did me; and so at last we were persuaded to buy the two gross between us." . . .

Our family had now made several vain attempts to be fine. "You see, my children," said I, "how little is to be got by attempts to impose upon the world. Those that are poor and will associate with none but the rich are hated by those they avoid, and despised by those they follow."

— Oliver Goldsmith.

A LEGEND OF BREGENZ

Girt round with rugged mountains
    The fair Lake Constance lies;
In her blue heart reflected,
    Shine back the starry skies;
And watching each white cloudlet
    Float silently and slow,
You think a piece of heaven
    Lies on our earth below!

Midnight is there: and silence
    Enthroned in heaven, looks down
Upon her own calm mirror,
    Upon a sleeping town;

For Bregenz, that quaint city
   Upon the Tyrol shore,
Has stood above Lake Constance
   A thousand years and more.

Her battlements and towers,
   Upon their rocky steep,
Have cast their trembling shadow
   For ages on the deep:
Mountain, and lake, and valley
   A sacred legend know,
Of how the town was saved one night
   Three hundred years ago.

Far from her home and kindred,
   A Tyrol maid had fled,
To serve in the Swiss valleys,
   And toil for daily bread;
And every year that fleeted
   So silently and fast,
Seemed to bear farther from her
   The memory of the past.

*   *   *   *   *

She spoke no more of Bregenz,
   With longing and with tears;
Her Tyrol home seemed faded
   In a deep mist of years;

She heeded not the rumors
   Of Austrian war and strife;
Each day she rose contented,
   To the calm toils of life.

*   *   *   *   *

And when at morn and evening
   She knelt before God's throne,
The accents of her childhood
   Rose to her lips alone.

And so she dwelt; the valley
   More peaceful year by year;
When suddenly strange portents
   Of some great deed seemed near.
The golden corn was bending
   Upon its fragile stalk,
While farmers, heedless of their fields,
   Paced up and down in talk.

The men seemed stern and altered,
   With looks cast on the ground;
With anxious faces, one by one
   The women gathered round;
All talk of flax, or spinning,
   Or work was put away;
The very children seemed afraid
   To go alone to play.

One day, out in the meadow
   With strangers from the town,
Some secret plan discussing,
   The men walked up and down.
Yet, now and then seemed watching,
   A strange uncertain gleam,
That looked like lances 'mid the trees,
   That stood below the stream.

At eve they all assembled,
   All care and doubt were fled;
With jovial laugh they feasted,
   The board was nobly spread.
The elder of the village
   Rose up, his glass in hand,
And cried, " We drink the downfall
   Of an accursed land !

" The night is growing darker,
   Ere one more day is flown,
Bregenz, our foeman's stronghold,
   Bregenz shall be our own ! "
The women shrank in terror
   (Yet Pride, too, had her part),
But one poor Tyrol maiden
   Felt death within her heart.

Before her, stood fair Bregenz,
  Once more her towers arose;
What were the friends beside her?
  Only her country's foes.
The faces of her kinsfolk,
  The days of childhood flown,
The echoes of her mountains
  Reclaimed her as their own!

Nothing she heard around her
  (Though shouts rang forth again),
Gone were the green Swiss valleys,
  The pasture and the plain;
Before her eyes one vision,
  And in her heart one cry,
That said, "Go forth, save Bregenz,
  And then, if need be, die!"

With trembling haste and breathless,
  With noiseless step she sped;
Horses and weary cattle
  Were standing in the shed;
She loosed the strong white charger
  That fed from out her hand,
She mounted, and she turned his head
  Towards her native land.

Out, out into the darkness —
    Faster, and still more fast;
The smooth grass flies behind her,
    The chestnut wood is past.

*   *   *   *   *

"Faster!" she cries, "O faster!"
    Eleven the church bells chime;
"O God," she cries, "help Bregenz,
    And bring me there in time!"
But louder than bells' ringing
    Or lowing of the kine,
Grows nearer in the midnight
    The rushing of the Rhine.
She strives to pierce the darkness,
    And looser throws the rein;
Her steed must breast the waters
    That dash above his mane.

*   *   *   *   *

They reached the gate of Bregenz
    Just as the midnight rings,
And out come serf and soldier
    To meet the news she brings.

Bregenz is saved! Ere daylight
    Her battlements are manned;
Defiance greets the army
    That marches on the land.

And if to deeds heroic
  Should endless fame be paid,
Bregenz does well to honor
  The noble Tyrol maid.

Three hundred years are vanished,
  And yet upon the hill
An old stone gateway rises
  To do her honor still.
And there, when Bregenz women
  Sit spinning in the shade,
They see in quaint old carving
  The charger and the maid.

And when, to guard old Bregenz
  By gateway, street, and tower,
The warder paces all night long,
  And calls each passing hour:
"Nine, ten, eleven," he cries aloud,
  And then (O crown of Fame!)
When midnight pauses in the skies
  He calls the maiden's name.
                    — Adelaide A. Procter.

PARABLES

ON PERSECUTION

1. And it came to pass, after these things, that Abraham sat in the door of his tent about the going down of the sun.

2. And behold a man, bowed with age, came from the way of the wilderness, leaning on a staff.

3. And Abraham rose and met him, and said, "Turn in, I pray thee, and wash thy feet, and tarry all night, and thou shalt arise early in the morning and go on thy way."

4. But the man said, " Nay, for I will abide under this tree."

5. And Abraham pressed him greatly; so he turned, and they went into the tent, and Abraham baked unleavened bread, and they did eat.

6. And when Abraham saw that the man blessed not God, he said unto him, " Wherefore dost thou not worship the most high God, creator of heaven and earth?"

7. And the man answered and said, " I do not worship the God thou speakest of, neither do I call upon his name; for I have made to myself a god, which abideth always in my house, and provideth me with all things."

8. And Abraham's zeal was kindled against the

man, and he arose and drove him forth with blows into the wilderness.

9. And at midnight God called upon Abraham saying, "Abraham, where is the stranger?"

10. And Abraham answered and said, "Lord, he would not worship thee, neither would he call upon thy name; therefore I have driven him out before my face into the wilderness."

11. And God said, "Have I borne with him these hundred ninety and eight years, and clothed him, notwithstanding his rebellion against me; and couldst not thou, that art thyself a sinner, bear with him one night?"

12. And Abraham said, "Let not the anger of the Lord wax hot against his servant; lo, I have sinned; forgive me, I pray thee."

13. And Abraham arose, and went forth into the wilderness, and sought diligently for the man, and found him, and returned with him to the tent; and when he had entreated him kindly, he sent him away on the morrow with gifts.

14. And God spake unto Abraham, saying, "For this thy sin shall thy seed be afflicted four hundred years in a strange land.

15. "But for thy repentance will I deliver them; and they shall come forth with power and gladness of heart, and with much substance."

ON BROTHERLY LOVE

1. In those days there was no worker of iron in all the land. And the merchants of Midian passed by with their camels, bearing spices, and myrrh, and balm, and wares of iron.

2. And Reuben bought an ax of the Ishmaelite merchants, which he prized highly, for there was none in his father's house.

3. And Simeon said unto Reuben his brother, "Lend me, I pray thee, thine ax." But he refused, and would not.

4. And Levi also said unto him, "My brother, lend me, I pray thee, thine ax;" and he refused him also.

5. Then came Judah unto Reuben, and entreated him, saying, "Lo, thou lovest me, and I have always loved thee; do not refuse me the use of thine ax."

6. But Reuben turned from him, and refused him likewise.

7. Now it came to pass that Reuben hewed timber on the bank of the river, and his ax fell therein, and he could by no means find it.

8. But Simeon, Levi, and Judah had sent a messenger after the Ishmaelites with money, and had bought for themselves each an ax.

9. Then came Reuben unto Simeon, and said, "Lo,

I have lost mine ax, and my work is unfinished; lend me thine, I pray thee."

10. And Simeon answered him, saying, "Thou wouldst not lend me thine ax, therefore will I not lend thee mine."

11. Then he went unto Levi, and said unto him, "My brother, thou knowest my loss and my necessity; lend me, I pray thee, thine ax."

12. And Levi reproached him, saying, "Thou wouldst not lend me thine ax when I desired it; but I will be better than thou, and will lend thee mine."

13. And Reuben was grieved at the rebuke of Levi, and, being ashamed, turned from him, and took not the ax, but sought his brother Judah.

14. And, as he drew near, Judah beheld his countenance as it were covered with grief and shame; and he prevented him, saying, "My brother, I know thy loss; but why should it trouble thee? Lo, have I not an ax that will serve both thee and me? Take it, I pray thee, and use it as thine own."

15. And Reuben fell on his neck, and kissed him, with tears, saying, "Thy kindness is great, but thy goodness in forgiving me is greater. Thou art indeed my brother, and whilst I live will I love thee."

16. And Judah said, "Let us also love our other brethren; behold, are we not all of one blood?"

17. And Joseph saw these things, and reported them to his father Jacob.

18. And Jacob said, "Reuben did wrong, but he repented; Simeon also did wrong; and Levi was not altogether blameless.

19. "But the heart of Judah is princely. Judah hath the soul of a king. His father's children shall bow down before him, and he shall rule over his brethren."
— BENJAMIN FRANKLIN.

NOBILITY

TRUE worth is in being, not seeing —
    In doing each day that goes by
Some little good — not in the dreaming
    Of great things to do by and by.
For whatever men say in their blindness,
    And spite of the fancies of youth,
There's nothing so kingly as kindness,
    And nothing so royal as truth.

We get back our mete as we measure —
    We cannot do wrong and feel right;
Nor can we give pain and gain pleasure,
    For justice avenges each slight.
The air for the wing of the sparrow,
    The bush for the robin and wren;
But always the path that is narrow
    And straight, for the children of men.

We cannot make bargains for blisses,
   Nor catch them like fishes in nets;
And sometimes the thing our life misses,
   Helps more than the thing that it gets.
For good lieth not in pursuing,
   Nor gaining of great or of small,
But just in the doing; and doing
   As we would be done by, is all.

Through envy, through malice, through hating,
   Against the world early and late,
No jot of our courage abating —
   Our part is to work and to wait.
And slight is the sting of his trouble
   Whose winnings are less than his worth;
For he who is honest is noble,
   Whatever his fortunes or birth.

— ALICE CARY.

TACT AND TALENT

TALENT is something, but tact is everything. Talent is serious, sober, grave, and respectable; tact is all that, and more too. It is not a sixth sense, but it is the life of all the five. It is the open eye, the quick ear, the judging taste, the keen smell, and the lively touch; it is the interpreter of all riddles, the surmounter of all difficulties, the remover of all obstacles. It is useful in all places, and at all times; it is useful in solitude, for it shows a man into the world; it is useful in society, for it shows him his way through the world.

Talent is power, tact is skill; talent is weight, tact is momentum; talent knows what to do, tact knows how to do it; talent makes a man respectable, tact will make him respected; talent is wealth, tact is ready money. For all the practical purposes, tact carries it against talent ten to one.

Take them to the theater, and put them against each other on the stage, and talent shall produce you a tragedy that shall scarcely live long enough to be condemned, while tact keeps the house in a roar, night after night, with its successful farces. There is no want of dramatic talent, there is no want of dramatic tact; but they are seldom together: so we have successful pieces which are not respectable, and respectable pieces which are not successful.

Take them to the bar, and let them shake their learned curls at each other in legal rivalry; talent sees its way clearly, but tact is first at its journey's end. Talent has many a compliment from the bench, but tact touches fees. Talent makes the world wonder that it gets on no faster, tact arouses astonishment that it gets on so fast. And the secret is, that it has no weight to carry; it makes no false steps;

it hits the right nail on the head; it loses no time; it takes all hints; and by keeping its eye on the weather-cock, is ready to take advantage of every wind that blows.

Take them into the church: talent has always something worth hearing, tact is sure of abundance of hearers; talent may obtain a living, tact will make one; talent gets a good name, tact a great one; talent convinces, tact converts; talent is an honor to the profession, tact gains honor from the profession.

Take them to court: talent feels its weight, tact finds its way; talent commands, tact is obeyed; talent is honored with approbation, and tact is blessed by preferment. Place them in the senate: talent has the ear of the house, but tact wins its heart, and has its votes; talent is fit for employment, but tact is fitted for it.

Tact seems to know everything, without learning anything. It has served an extemporary apprenticeship; it wants no drilling; it never ranks in the awkward squad; it has no left hand, no deaf ear, no blind side. It puts on no look of wondrous wisdom, it has no air of profundity, but plays with the details of place as dexterously as a well-taught hand flourishes over the keys of the pianoforte.

From " London Atlas."

THE MAN WITHOUT A COUNTRY

PHILIP NOLAN was as fine a young officer as there was in the "Legion of the West," as the western division of our army was then called. When Aaron Burr made his first dashing expedition down to New Orleans, he met this gay, bright young fellow. Burr marked him, talked to him, walked with him, took him a day or two's voyage in his flatboat, and, in short, fascinated him. Under this baneful influence poor Nolan became sick of the service and in time turned traitor to his country. He was tried before a court martial for treason, and found guilty enough; yet you and I would never have heard of him, reader, but that when the president of the court asked him if he wished to say anything to show that he had always been faithful to the United States, he cried out in a fit of frenzy:—

"Curse the United States! I wish I may never hear of the United States again!"

I suppose he did not know how the words shocked old Colonel Morgan, who was holding the court. Half the officers who sat in it had served through the Revolution, and their lives, not to say their necks, had been risked for the very idea which he so cavalierly cursed in his madness.

Old Morgan was, indeed, terribly shocked. If

Nolan had compared George Washington to Benedict Arnold, or had cried, "God save King George," Morgan would not have felt worse. He called the court into his private room, and returned in fifteen minutes, with a face like a sheet, to say:—

"Prisoner, hear the sentence of the Court! The Court decides, subject to the approval of the President, that you never hear the name of the United States again."

Nolan laughed. But nobody else laughed. Old Morgan was too solemn, and the whole room was hushed dead as night for a minute.

Then Morgan added,—"Mr. Marshal, take the prisoner to Orleans in an armed boat, and deliver him to the naval commander there." The marshal gave his orders and the prisoner was taken out of court.

"Mr. Marshal," continued old Morgan, "see that no one mentions the United States to the prisoner. Mr. Marshal, make my respects to Lieutenant Mitchell at Orleans, and request him to order that no one shall mention the United States to the prisoner while he is on board ship. The Court is adjourned without day."

President Jefferson approved the sentence of the court, and Philip Nolan was a man without a country. The secretary of the navy was requested to put him on board a government vessel, and to direct that under no circumstances was the prisoner ever to hear of his country or to see any information regarding it. Otherwise he had the freedom of the ship on which he was confined. No mess liked to have him permanently, because his presence cut off all talk of home, or of the prospect of return, of politics or letters, of peace or of war, — cut off more than half the talk men liked to have at sea.

As he was almost never permitted to go on shore, even though the vessel lay in port for months, his time at the best hung heavy; and everybody was permitted to lend him books, if they were not published in America and made no allusion to it. He had almost all the foreign papers that came into the ship, sooner or later; only somebody must go over them first, and cut out any advertisement or stray paragraph that alluded to America. Among these books was the "Lay of the Last Minstrel," which they had all of them heard of, but which most of them had never seen. Nobody thought there could be any risk of anything national in that, so Nolan was permitted to join the circle one afternoon when a lot of them sat on deck smoking and reading aloud.

Well, it so happened that in his turn Nolan took the book and read to the others; and he read very well. No one in the circle knew a line of the poem, only it was all magic and Border chivalry, and was ten thousand years ago. Poor Nolan read steadily through the fifth canto, stopped a minute and drank something, and then began, without a thought of what was coming, —

> "Breathes there the man with soul so dead,
> Who never to himself hath said," —

It seems impossible to us that anybody ever heard this for the first time; but all these fellows did then, and poor Nolan himself went on, —

> "This is my own, my native land!"

Then they all saw that something was to pay; but he expected to get through, I suppose, turned a little pale, but plunged on, —

> "Whose heart hath ne'er within him burned,
> As home his footsteps he hath turned
> From wandering on a foreign strand? —
> If such there breathe, go, mark him well," —

By this time the men were all beside themselves, wishing there was any way to make him turn over two pages; but he had not quite presence of mind for that; he colored crimson, and staggered on, —

> "For him no minstrel raptures swell;
> High though his titles, proud his name,
> Boundless his wealth as wish can claim,
> Despite these titles, power, and pelf,
> The wretch, concentred all in self," —

and here the poor fellow choked, could not go on, but started up, slung the book into the sea, vanished into his stateroom, and we did not see him for two months again.

He never read aloud again unless it was the Bible or Shakespeare, or something else he was sure of. But it was not that merely. He never entered in with the other young men exactly as a companion again. He was always shy afterward, very seldom spoke, unless he was spoken to, except to a very few friends.

A happier story than this one I have told is of the war which came along soon after. In one of the great frigate duels with the English, it happened that a round shot from the enemy entered one of our ports square, and took right down the officer of the gun himself, and almost every man of the gun's crew. Now you may say what you choose about courage, but that is not a nice thing to see. But, as the men who were not killed picked themselves up, and as they and the surgeon's people were carrying off the bodies, there appeared Nolan, in his shirt sleeves, with the rammer in his hand; and, just as if he had been the officer, told them off with authority, and with that way which makes men feel sure all is right and is going to be right. And he finished loading the gun with his own hands, aimed it, and bade the men fire. And there he stayed, in command of that gun, keeping those fellows in spirits, till the enemy struck. The captain walked forward by way of encouraging the men, and Nolan touched his hat and said: —

"I am showing them how we do this in the artillery, sir."

"I see you are, and I thank you, sir; and I shall never forget this day, sir, and you never shall, sir," said the captain.

And after the whole thing was over, and he had the Englishman's sword, in the midst of the state and ceremony of the quarter-deck, the captain said: —

"Where is Mr. Nolan? Ask Mr. Nolan to come here."

And when Nolan came, he said: "Mr. Nolan, we are all very grateful to you to-day; you are one of us to-day; you will be named in the dispatches."

And then the old man took off his own sword of ceremony, and gave it to Nolan, and made him put it on. Nolan cried like a baby, and well he might. He had not worn a sword since that wretched day at Fort Adams.

The captain did mention him in the dispatches. It was always said he asked that Nolan might be pardoned. He wrote a special letter to the secretary of war, but nothing ever came of it.

My own acquaintance with Philip Nolan began six or eight years after the English war, on my first voyage after I was appointed a midshipman. We had him to dine in our mess once a week, and the caution was given that on that day nothing was to be said about home. I did not ask why; there were a great many things which seemed to me to have as little reason.

I first came to understand about "the man without a country" one day when we overhauled a dirty little schooner which had slaves on board. An officer was sent to take charge of her, and, after a few minutes, he sent back his boat to ask that some one might be sent who could speak Portuguese. Nolan stepped out and said he should be glad to interpret, as he understood the language.

"Tell them they are free," said Vaughan.

Nolan put that into such Portuguese as the negroes could understand. Then there was a yell of delight, leaping and dancing, kissing of Nolan's feet.

"Tell them," said Vaughan, well pleased, "that I will take them all to Cape Palmas."

This did not answer so well. Cape Palmas was far from the homes of most of them, and their interpreters instantly said, "*Ah, non Palmas.*" Vaughan asked Nolan eagerly what they said. The drops stood on poor Nolan's white forehead, as he said: —

"He says, 'Not Palmas.' He says, 'Take us home, take us to our own country, take us to our own house, take us to our own pickaninnies and our own women.' He says he has an old father and mother who will die if they do not see him. And this one says he left his people all sick, and paddled down to Fernando to beg the white doctor to come and help them, and that they caught him in the bay just in sight of home, and that he has never seen anybody from home since then. And this one says," choked out Nolan, "that he has not heard a word from his home in six months, while he has been locked up in a barracoon."

As quick as Vaughan could get words, he said: —

"Tell them yes, yes, yes; tell them they shall go to the Mountains of the Moon, if they will. If I sail the schooner through the Great White Desert, they shall go home!"

And after some fashion Nolan said so. And then they all fell to kissing him again, and wanted to rub his nose with theirs.

But he could not stand it long; and getting Vaughan to say he might go back, he beckoned me down into our boat. As we lay back in the stern sheets and the men gave way he said to me: "Youngster, let that show you what it is to be without a family, without a home, and without a country. And if you are ever tempted to say a word or to do a thing that shall put a bar between you and your family, your home, and your country, pray God in His mercy to take you that instant home to His own heaven. Stick by your family, boy; forget you have a self, while you do everything for them. Think of your home, boy; write and send, and talk about it. Let it be nearer and nearer to your thought, the farther you have to travel from it; and rush back to it when you are free, as that poor black slave is doing now. And for your country, boy," and the words rattled in his throat, "and for that flag," and he pointed to the ship, "never dream a dream but of serving her as she bids you, though the service carry you through a thousand hells. No matter what happens to you, no matter who flatters you or abuses you, never look at another flag, never let a night pass but you pray God to bless that flag. Remember, boy, that behind all these men you have to do with, behind officers, and government, and people even, there is the Country Herself, your Country, and that you belong to her as you belong to your own mother."

I was frightened by his calm, hard passion; but I blundered out that I would, by all that was holy, and that I had never thought of doing anything else. He hardly seemed to hear me; but he did, almost in a whisper say: " Oh, if anybody had said so to me when I was of your age!"

When we parted from him at the end of our cruise, I was more sorry than I can tell. I was glad to meet him once more in 1830, but after that I never saw him again. And now it seems the dear old fellow is dead. He has found a home at last, and a country.

Since writing this, I have received a letter which gives an account of Nolan's last hours. Here is an extract from the letter: —

LEVANT, 2° 2' S. 131° W.

DEAR FRED: — I try to find heart and life to tell you that it is all over with dear old Nolan. I could see that he was not strong, but I had no idea the end was so near. He had let the doctor come and see him as he lay there,—the first time the doctor had been in the stateroom,—and he said he should like to see me. Well, I went in, and there, to be sure, the poor fellow lay in his berth, smiling pleasantly as he gave me his hand, but looking very frail. I could not help a glance round, which showed me what a little shrine he had made of the box he was lying in. The stars and stripes were triced up above and around a picture of Washington, and he had painted a majestic eagle, with lightnings blazing from his beak and his foot just clasping the whole globe, which his wings overshadowed. The dear old boy saw my glance, and said, with a sad smile, "Here, you see, I have a country!"

And he said, "Look in my Bible, when I am gone." And I went away. I had no thought it was the end. But in an hour, when the doctor went in gently, he found Nolan had breathed his life away with a smile.

We looked in his Bible, and there was a slip of paper at the place where he had marked the text:—

"They desire a country, even a heavenly: wherefore God is not ashamed to be called their God: for He hath prepared for them a city."

On this slip of paper he had written:—

"Bury me in the sea; it has been my home, and I love it. But will not some one set up a stone for my memory at Fort Adams or at Orleans, that my disgrace may not be more than I ought to bear? Say on it:—

"IN MEMORY OF

"PHILIP NOLAN

"*Lieutenant in the Army of the United States*

"He loved his country as no other man has loved her; but no man deserved less at her hands."

— EDWARD EVERETT HALE (*Abridged*).

THE BATTLE OF LEXINGTON.

THE BATTLE OF LEXINGTON

AT two in the morning of April 19, 1775, under the eye of the minister, and of Hancock and Adams, Lexington common was alive with the minutemen; and not with them only, but with the old men, who were exempts, except in case of immediate danger to the town. The roll was called, and of the militia and alarm men, about one hundred and thirty answered to their names. The captain, John Parker, ordered every one to load with powder and ball, but to take care not to be the first to fire. Messengers, sent to look for the British regulars, reported that there were no signs of their approach. A watch was therefore set, and the company dismissed with orders to come together at beat of drum. Some went to their own homes; some to the tavern, near the southeast corner of the common. Samuel Adams and Hancock, whose seizure was believed to be intended, were persuaded to retire toward Woburn.

The last stars were vanishing from night, when the foremost party, led by Pitcairn, a major of marines, was discovered, advancing quickly and in silence. Alarm guns were fired, and the drums beat, not a call to village husbandmen, only, but the reveille to humanity. Less than seventy, perhaps less than sixty, obeyed the summons, and in sight of half as many boys and unarmed men, were paraded in two ranks, a few rods north of the meetinghouse.

How often in that building had they, with renewed professions of their faith, looked up to God as the stay of their fathers and the protector of their privileges! How often on that green, hard by the burial place of their forefathers, had they pledged themselves to each other to combat manfully for their birthright inheritance of liberty! There they now stood side by side, under the provincial banner, with arms in their hands, silent and fearless, willing to shed their blood for their rights, scrupulous not to begin civil war. The ground on which they trod was the altar of freedom, and they were to furnish the victims.

The British van, hearing the drum and the alarm guns, halted to load; the remaining companies came up; and, at half an hour before sunrise, the advance party hurried forward at double quick time, almost upon a run, closely followed by the grenadiers. Pitcairn rode in front, and when within five or six rods of the minutemen, cried out: "Disperse, ye villains! ye rebels, disperse! lay down your arms! why don't you lay down arms and disperse?"

The main part of the countrymen stood motionless in the ranks, witnesses against aggression; too few to resist, too brave to fly. At this, Pitcairn discharged a pistol, and with a loud voice cried, "Fire!"

The order was followed first by a few guns, which did no execution, and then by a close and deadly discharge of musketry.

In the disparity of numbers, Parker ordered his men to disperse. Then, and not till then, did a few of them, on their own impulse, return the British fire. These random shots of fugitives or dying men did no harm, except that Pitcairn's horse was perhaps grazed, and a private of the Tenth Light Infantry was touched slightly in the leg.

Jonas Parker, the strongest and best wrestler in Lexington, had promised never to run from British troops; and he kept his vow. A wound brought him to his knees. Having discharged his gun, he was preparing to load it again, when he was stabbed by a bayonet, and lay on the post which he took at the morning drum-beat. So fell Isaac Muzzey, and so died the aged Robert Munroe, who, in 1758, had been an ensign at Louisburg. Jonathan Harrington, junior, was struck in front of his own house on the north of the common. His wife was at the window as he fell. With blood gushing from his breast, he rose in her sight, tottered, fell again, then crawled on hands and knees toward his dwelling; she ran to meet him, but only reached him as he expired on their threshold. Caleb Harrington, who had gone into the meetinghouse for powder, was shot as he came out. Samuel Hadley and John Brown were pursued, and killed, after they left the green. Asahel Porter of Woburn, who had been taken prisoner by the British on the march, endeavoring to escape, was shot within a few rods of the common. Seven men of Lexington were killed, nine wounded, — a quarter part of all who stood in arms upon the green.

Day came in all the beauty of an early spring. The trees were budding; the grass growing rankly a full month before its time; the bluebird and the robin gladdening the genial season, and calling forth the beams of the sun which on that morning shone with the warmth of summer; but distress and horror gathered over the inhabitants of the peaceful town. There on the green lay in death the gray-haired and the young, the grassy field was red "with the innocent blood of their brethren slain," crying unto God for vengeance from the ground.

These are the village heroes, who were more than of noble birth, proving by their spirit that they were of a race divine. They gave their lives in testimony to the rights of mankind, bequeathing to their country an assurance of success in the mighty struggle which they began.

— GEORGE BANCROFT.

LEXINGTON

SLOWLY the mist o'er the meadow was creeping,
   Bright on the dewy buds glistened the sun,
When from his couch, while his children were sleeping,
   Rose the bold rebel and shouldered his gun.
        Waving her golden veil
        Over the silent dale,
Blithe looked the morning on cottage and spire;
        Hushed was his parting sigh,
        While from his noble eye
Flashed the last sparkle of liberty's fire.

On the smooth green, where the fresh leaf is springing,
   Calmly the first-born of glory have met.
Hark! the death volley around them is ringing!
   Look! with their lifeblood the young grass is wet!
        Faint is the feeble breath
        Murmuring low in death, —
"Tell to our sons how their fathers have died."
        Nerveless the iron hand,
        Raised for its native land,
Lies by the weapon that gleams at its side.

Over the hillsides the wild knell is tolling,
   From their far hamlets the yeomanry come;
As through the storm clouds the thunder-burst rolling,
   Circles the beat of the mustering drum.

   Fast on the soldier's path
   Darken the waves of wrath;
Long have they gathered, and loud shall they fall;
   Red glares the musket's flash,
   Sharp rings the rifle's crash,
Blazing and clanging from thicket and wall.

Gayly the plume of the horseman was dancing,
 Never to shadow his cold brow again;
Proudly at morning the war steed was prancing;
 Reeking and panting he droops on the rein;
   Pale is the lip of scorn,
   Voiceless the trumpet horn,
Torn is the silken-fringed red cross on high;
   Many a belted breast
   Low on the turf shall rest,
Ere the dark hunters the herd have passed by.

Snow-girdled crags where the hoarse wind is raving,
 Rocks where the weary floods murmur and wail,
Wilds where the fern by the furrow is waving,
 Reeled with the echoes that rode on the gale;
   Far as the tempest thrills
   Over the darkened hills,
Far as the sunshine streams over the plain,
   Roused by the tyrant band,
   Woke all the mighty land,
Girded for battle, from mountain to main.

Green be the graves where her martyrs are lying!
　Shroudless and tombless they sank to their rest, —
While o'er their ashes the starry fold flying
　Wraps the proud eagle they roused from his nest!
　　Borne on her northern pine,
　　Long o'er the foaming brine,
Spread her broad banner to storm and to sun;
　　Heaven keep her ever free,
　　Wide as o'er land and sea
Floats the fair emblem her heroes have won!
　　　　　　　—OLIVER WENDELL HOLMES.

THE BELL OF LIBERTY

THE representatives of the people assembled in solemn conclave, and long and anxiously surveyed the perilous ground on which they were treading. To recede was now impossible; to go on seemed fraught with terrible consequences. The result of the long and fearful conflict that must follow was more than doubtful. For twenty days Congress was tossed on a sea of perplexity.

At length, Richard Henry Lee, shaking off the fetters that galled his noble spirit, arose on the 7th of June, and in a clear, deliberate tone, every accent of which rang to the farthest extremity of the silent hall, proposed the following resolution: "*Resolved*, That these United Colonies are, and ought to be, free and independent States, and all political connection between us and the States of Great Britain is, and ought to be, totally dissolved."

John Adams, in whose soul glowed the burning future, seconded the resolution in a speech so full of impassioned fervor, thrilling eloquence, and prophetic power that Congress was carried away before it, as by a resistless wave. The die was cast, and every man was now compelled to meet the issue. The resolution was finally deferred till the 1st of July, to allow a committee, appointed for that purpose, to draft a Declaration of Independence.

When the day arrived, the Declaration was taken up and debated, article by article. The discussion continued for three days, and was characterized by great excitement. At length, the various sections having been gone through with, the next day, July 4th, was appointed for action.

It was soon known throughout the city; and in the morning, before Congress assembled, the streets were filled with excited men, some gathered in groups, engaged in eager discussion, and others moving toward the State House. All business was forgotten in the momentous crisis which the country had now reached.

No sooner had the members taken their seats than the multitude gathered in a dense mass around the entrance. The bellman mounted to the belfry, to be ready to proclaim the joyful tidings of freedom as soon as the final vote was passed. A bright-eyed boy was stationed below to give the signal.

Around the bell, brought from England, had been cast more than twenty years before the prophetic motto: —

"PROCLAIM LIBERTY THROUGHOUT ALL THE LAND UNTO ALL THE INHABITANTS THEREOF."

Although its loud clang had often sounded over the city, the proclamation engraved on its iron lip had never yet been spoken aloud.

It was expected that the final vote would be taken without delay; but hour after hour wore on, and no report came from that mysterious hall where the fate of a continent was in suspense. The multitude grew impatient; the old man leaned over the railing, straining his eyes downward, till his heart misgave him and hope yielded to fear.

But at length, at about two o'clock, the door of the hall opened, and a voice exclaimed, "It has passed." The word leapt like lightning from lip to lip, followed by huzzas that shook the building. The boy-sentinel turned to the belfry, clapped his hands, and shouted, "Ring! ring!"

The desponding bellman, electrified into life by the

joyful news, seized the iron tongue, and hurled it backward and forward with a clang that startled every heart in Philadelphia like a bugle blast. "Clang! clang!" the bell of Liberty resounded on, higher and clearer, and more joyous, blending in its deep and thrilling vibrations, and proclaiming in loud and long accents over all the land, the motto that encircled it.

Glad messengers caught the tidings as they floated out on the air, and sped off in every direction to bear them onward. When they reached New York, the bells rang out the glorious news, and the excited multitude, surging hither and thither, at length gathered around the Bowling Green, and, seizing the leaden statue of George III, which stood there, tore it into fragments. These were afterward run into bullets, and hurled against his Majesty's troops.

When the Declaration arrived in Boston, the people gathered to old Faneuil Hall to hear it read; and as the last sentence fell from the lips of the reader, a loud shout went up, and soon from every fortified height and every battery the thunder of cannon re-echoed the joy.

— J. T. Headley.

THE RISING IN 1776

Out of the North the wild news came,
Far flashing on its wings of flame,
Swift as the boreal light which flies
At midnight through the startled skies.
And there was tumult in the air,
   The fife's shrill note, the drum's loud beat,
And through the wide land everywhere
   The answering tread of hurrying feet;
While the first oath of Freedom's gun
Came on the blast from Lexington;
And Concord, roused, no longer tame,
Forgot her old baptismal name,
Made bare her patriot arm of power,
And swelled the discord of the hour.

Within its shade of elm and oak
   The church of Berkley Manor stood;
There Sunday found the rural folk,
   And some esteemed of gentle blood.
   In vain their feet with loitering tread
Passed 'mid the graves where rank is naught;
All could not read the lesson taught
   In that republic of the dead.

How sweet the hour of Sabbath talk,
   The vale with peace and sunshine full
Where all the happy people walk,

Decked in their homespun flax and wool!
Where youth's gay hats with blossoms bloom;
And every maid with simple art,
Wears on her breast, like her own heart,
A bud whose depths are all perfume;
While every garment's gentle stir
Is breathing rose and lavender.

The pastor came; his snowy locks
Hallowed his brow of thought and care;
And calmly, as shepherds lead their flocks,
He led into the house of prayer.
The pastor rose; the prayer was strong;
The psalm was warrior David's song;
The text, a few short words of might, —
"The Lord of hosts shall arm the right!"

He spoke of wrongs too long endured,
Of sacred rights to be secured;
Then from his patriot tongue of flame
The startling words for Freedom came.
The stirring sentences he spake
Compelled the heart to glow or quake,
And, rising on his theme's broad wing,
And grasping in his nervous hand
The imaginary battle brand,
In face of death he dared to fling
Defiance to a tyrant king.

And there the startling drum and fife
Fired the living with fiercer life;
While overhead, with wild increase,
Forgetting its ancient toll of peace,
  The great bell swung as ne'er before:
It seemed as it would never cease;
And every word its ardor flung
From off its jubilant iron tongue
  Was, "WAR! WAR! WAR!"

"Who dares?" — this was the patriot's cry,
As striding from the desk he came, —
  "Come out with me, in Freedom's name,
For her to live, for her to die?"
A hundred hands flung up reply,
A hundred voices answered, "*I!*"
                      — THOMAS BUCHANAN READ.

RALEIGH AND QUEEN ELIZABETH

AT this moment the gates opened and ushers came forth in array. After these, amid a crowd of lords and ladies, — so placed around her that she could see and be seen on all sides, — came Elizabeth herself. She was then in the full glow of what in a sovereign was called beauty, and possessed a noble figure joined to striking and commanding features.

Young Walter Raleigh had never before been so near the person of the Queen, and he pressed forward as far as the line of guards permitted. Unbonneting, at the same time he fixed his eager gaze on the Queen's approach with a mixture of respectful curiosity and modest, yet ardent admiration. Walter then withdrew.

The guards, struck with his rich attire and noble countenance, allowed him to approach the ground over which the Queen was to pass, somewhat closer than was permitted to ordinary spectators.

Thus the adventurous youth stood full in Elizabeth's eye, and she fixed her keen glance on Walter as she approached the place where he stood. Just then there occurred an incident that drew her attention toward him yet more strongly.

The night had been rainy, and just where the young gentleman stood a small quantity of mud interrupted the Queen's passage. As she hesitated to pass on, Walter, snatching his cloak from his shoulder, threw it on the miry spot so as to insure her stepping over it without soiling her feet.

Elizabeth looked at the young man, who accompanied this act of devoted courtesy with a profound reverence, and a blush that overspread his whole countenance. The Queen was confused, and blushed in her turn, nodded her head, and hastily passed on, and embarked in her barge without saying a word.

"Come along, Sir Coxcomb," said Walter's companion, Blount; "your gay mantle will need the brush to-day, I fancy."

"This cloak," said the youth, taking it up and folding it, "shall never be brushed while in my possession."

"And that will not be long, if you have not a little more economy," muttered Blount.

Their conversation was here interrupted by one of

the royal attendants. "I was sent," said he, after looking at Blount and Walter attentively, "to a gentleman who hath no cloak or a muddy one. You, sir, I think," addressing the younger cavalier, "are the man: you will please follow me."

The young cavalier was then guided to the water side by the attendant, who showed him marked respect. He ushered Raleigh into one of the skiffs that lay ready to attend the Queen's barge, which was already proceeding up the river.

The two rowers used their oars with such skill that they very soon brought their little skiff under the stern of the Queen's barge. Here Elizabeth sat beneath an awning, attended by two or three ladies and the nobles of her household. She looked more than once at the boat in which the young adventurer was seated, spoke to those around her, and seemed to laugh.

At length one of the attendants, by the Queen's order apparently, made a sign for the young man to step from his own skiff into the royal barge. This he did with graceful agility at the fore part of the boat, and was brought aft to the Queen's presence.

Raleigh underwent the gaze of majesty, not the less gracefully that his self-possession was mingled with embarrassment. The muddied cloak still hung upon his arm, and formed the natural topic with which the Queen introduced the conversation.

"You have this day spoiled a gay mantle in our service, young man. We thank you for your service, though the manner of offering it was unusual and somewhat bold."

"In a sovereign's need," answered Walter, "it is each liegeman's duty to be bold."

"That was well spoken, my lord," said the Queen, turning to a grave person who sat beside her. "Well, young man, your gallantry shall not pass unrewarded. Go to the wardrobe-keeper, and he shall have orders to supply the suit which you have cast away in our service. Thou shalt have a suit, and that of the newest cut, I promise thee, on the word of a princess."

"May it please your Grace," said Walter, hesitating, "it is not for so humble a servant of your Majesty to measure out your bounties; but if it became me to choose —"

"Thou wouldst have gold, I warrant me," said the Queen, interrupting him. "Fie, young man! Yet thou mayest be poor," she added, "or thy parents may be. It shall be gold, if thou wilt."

Walter waited patiently until the Queen had done, and then modestly assured her that gold was still less in his wish than the raiment her Majesty had before offered.

"How, boy," said the Queen, "neither gold nor

garment? What is it thou wouldst have of me, then?"

"Only permission, madam, to wear the cloak which did you this trifling service."

"Permission to wear thine own cloak, thou silly boy!" said the Queen.

"It is no longer mine," said Walter. "When your Majesty's foot touched it, it became a fit mantle for a prince, but far too rich a one for its former owner."

The Queen again blushed, and sought to cover by laughing a slight degree of not unpleasant surprise and confusion.

"Heard you ever the like, my lords? The youth's head is turned with reading romances. I must know something of him, that I may send him safe to his friends. — What is thy name and birth?"

"Raleigh is my name, most gracious Queen; the youngest son of a large but honorable family of Devonshire."

"Raleigh?" said Elizabeth, after a moment's thought: "have we not heard of your service in Ireland?"

"I have been so fortunate as to do some service there, madam," replied Raleigh; "scarce, however, of importance enough to reach your Grace's ears."

"They hear farther than you think of, and have

heard of a youth who defended a ford in Shannon against a whole band of rebels, until the stream ran purple with their blood and his own."

"Some blood I may have lost," said the youth, looking down; "but it was where my best is due, and that is in your Majesty's service."

The Queen paused, and then said hastily, "You are very young to have fought so well and to speak so well. So hark ye, Master Raleigh, see thou fail not to wear thy muddy cloak, till our pleasure be further known. And here," she added, giving him a jewel of gold, "I give thee this to wear at the collar."

Raleigh, to whom nature had taught these courtly arts which many scarcely acquire from long experience, knelt, and, as he took from her hand the jewel, kissed the fingers which gave it.

— SIR WALTER SCOTT.

From "Kenilworth."

SILAS MARNER AND EPPIE

IN the early years of this century a linen weaver, named Silas Marner, worked at his vocation in a stone cottage near the village of Raveloe, not far from the edge of a deserted stone pit.

The years rolled on without producing any change in the life of Silas Marner and his neighbors. There was only one important addition which the years had brought: it was that Master Marner had laid by a fine sight of money somewhere.

Gradually the guineas, the crowns, and the half-crowns grew to a heap, and Silas began to think the money was conscious of him and he would on no account have exchanged those coins, which had become his familiars, for other coins with unknown faces. He handled them, he counted them; but it was only in the night, when his work was done, that he drew them out to enjoy their companionship. He had taken up some bricks in his floor underneath his loom, and here he had made a hole in which he set the iron pot that contained his guineas and silver coins, covering the bricks with sand whenever he replaced them.

So, year after year Silas Marner had lived in solitude, his guineas rising in the iron pot and his life narrowing and hardening.

But about the Christmas of the fifteenth year, after he came to Raveloe, a great change came over Marner's life.

One night, as he was about to sit down to his evening meal, Silas remembered that a bit of very fine twine was indispensable to a new piece of work, so taking up his lantern and his old sack, he left his cottage and set out on his errand. Returning from the village, he reached his door in much satisfaction that his errand was done. He opened it, and to his short-sighted eyes everything remained as he had left it except that the fire sent out a welcome increase of heat.

As soon as he was warm, he began to think that it would be a long time to wait till after supper before he drew out his guineas, and that it would be pleasant to see them on the table before him as he ate. He rose and placed his candle on the floor near his loom, swept away the sand and removed the bricks. The hole was empty! His heart beat violently, but the belief that his gold was gone could not come at once. He passed his trembling hand all about the hole, trying to think it possible that his eye had deceived him; then he held the candle in the hole, and examined it curiously, trembling more and more.

At last he shook so violently that he let fall the candle, and lifted his hands to his head, trying to steady himself that he might think. Had he put the gold somewhere else last night and then forgotten it? He searched in every corner; he turned his bed over and shook it; he looked in his brick oven where he laid his sticks. When, at length, there was no other place to be searched he kneeled down again and felt once more all around the hole.

His gold was not there. There was no shelter from the terrible truth.

One night, some weeks later, Silas stood in the doorway of his cottage, looking out at the wintry sky. Since he had lost his money he had contracted the habit of opening the door and looking out from time to time as if he thought that his money might be somehow coming back to him. Since the oncoming of twilight he had opened his door again and again, though only to shut it immediately at seeing all distance veiled by the falling snow. But the last time he opened it the snow had ceased, and the clouds were parting here and there. He stood and listened, and gazed for a long while, his heart touched with the chill of despair. He went in again, and put his right hand on the latch of the door to close it — but he did not close it. A strange wave of unconsciousness passed over him, and he stood like a graven image with wide but sightless eyes, holding open his door.

When Marner's sensibility returned, he closed his door, unaware of any change except that the light had grown dim, and that he was chilled and faint. He thought he had been too long standing at the door and looking out. Turning towards the hearth where the two logs had fallen apart and sent forth only a red, uncertain glimmer, he seated himself on his fireside chair and was stooping to push his logs together, when to his blurred vision it seemed as if there were gold on the floor in front of the hearth.

Gold! — his own gold — brought back to him as mysteriously as it had been taken away! He felt his heart begin to beat violently, and for a few moments he was unable to stretch out his hand and

grasp the restored treasure. The heap of gold seemed to glow and get larger beneath his agitated gaze. He leaned forward at last and stretched forth his hand; but instead of the hard coin, his fingers encountered soft, warm curls. In utter amazement, Silas fell on his knees to examine the marvel; it was a sleeping child — a round, fair thing with soft, yellow rings all over its head.

There was a cry on the hearth — the child had awakened, and Marner stooped to lift it on his knee. It clung around his neck and burst loud and louder into cries, in the bewilderment of waking. Silas pressed it to him, and almost unconsciously uttered sounds of hushing tenderness while he bethought himself that some of his porridge which had got cool by the dying fire, would do to feed the child, if it were only warmed up a little.

The porridge stopped the cries of the little one and made her lift her blue eyes with a wide, quiet gaze at Silas, as he put the spoon into her mouth. Presently she slipped from his knee and began to toddle about, but with a pretty stagger that made Silas jump up and follow her, lest she should fall against anything that would hurt her.

It seemed to Silas that this little girl had been sent to him in some mysterious way, to take the place of his lost gold, and he determined to keep her for his own, naming her Eppie after his mother. As the weeks grew to months, the child created fresh and fresh links between his life and the lives of his neighbors from which he had before shrunk continually.

Unlike the gold which needed nothing, Eppie was a creature of endless claims and ever growing desires, seeking and loving sunshine, and living sounds and living movements, and stirring the human kindness in all eyes that looked on her. When the sunshine grew strong and lasting, so that the buttercups were thick in the meadows, Silas might be seen in the sunny midday or in the late afternoon, strolling out to carry Eppie beyond the stone pits to where the flowers grew, till they reached some favorite bank where he could sit down while Eppie toddled to pluck the flowers and make remarks to the winged things that murmured happily above the bright petals.

By the time Eppie was three years old, she developed a fine capacity for mischief and for devising ingenious ways of being troublesome, which found much exercise not only for Silas's patience but for his watchfulness and penetration.

For example. He had wisely chosen a broad strip of linen as a means of fastening her to his loom when he was busy. It made a broad belt around her waist and was long enough to allow of her reaching her bed, but not long enough for her to attempt any dangerous climbing. One bright summer's morning Silas had been more engrossed than usual in "setting up" a new piece of work, an occasion on which his scissors were in requisition. These scissors had been kept carefully out of Eppie's reach, but the click of them had a peculiar attraction for her ear. Silas had seated himself at his loom, and the noise of weaving had begun; but he had left his scissors on a ledge which Eppie's arm was long enough to reach; and now, like a small mouse, watching her opportunity, she stole quietly from her corner, secured the scissors and toddled back to the bed again. She had a distinct intention as to the use of the scissors; and having cut the linen strip in a jagged but effectual manner, in two moments she had run out at the open door where the sunshine was inviting her, while poor Silas believed her to be a better child than usual. It was not until he happened to need his scissors that the terrible fact burst upon him: Eppie had run out by herself — had perhaps fallen into the stone pit. Silas, shaken by the worst fear that could have befallen him, rushed out, calling "Eppie," and ran eagerly about the uninclosed space exploring the dry cavities into which she might have fallen, and then gazing with questioning dread at the smooth, red surface of the water in the stone pit. The cold drops stood on his brow. How long had she been out? The meadow was searched in vain; and he got over the stile into the next field, looking with dying hope toward a small pond which was now reduced to its summer shallowness, so as to leave a wide margin of good adhesive mud. Here, however, sat Eppie, discoursing cheerfully to her own small boot, which she was using as a bucket to convey the water into a deep hoof mark, while her little naked foot was planted comfortably on a cushion of olive-green mud.

Here was clearly a case which demanded severe treatment, but Silas overcome with joy at finding his treasure again could do nothing but snatch her up and cover her with half-sobbing kisses. It was not until he had carried her home and had begun to think of the necessary washing, that he recollected the need that he should punish Eppie and "make her remember." The idea that she might run away and come to harm, gave him unusual resolution and for the first time he determined to try the coal hole — a small closet near the hearth.

"Naughty, naughty Eppie," he suddenly began, holding her on his knee and pointing to her muddy feet and clothes. "Naughty to cut with the scissors and run away. Eppie must go into the coal hole for being naughty. Daddy must put her in the coal hole." He half expected that this would be shock enough, and that Eppie would begin to cry. But instead of that she began to shake herself on his knee, as if the proposition opened a pleasing novelty. Seeing that he must proceed to extremities, he put her into the coal hole, and held the door closed with the trembling sense that he was using a strong measure. For a moment there was silence, but then came a little cry "Opy, opy!" and Silas let her out again, saying, "Now Eppie 'ull never be naughty again, else she must go in the coal hole — a black, naughty place."

The weaving must stand still a long while this morning, for now Eppie must be washed, and have clean clothes on; but it was to be hoped that this punishment would have a lasting effect, and save time in future. In half an hour she was clean again, and Silas, having turned his back to see what he could do with the linen band, threw it down again, with the reflection that Eppie would be good without fastening for the rest of the morning. He turned round again, and was going to place her in her little chair near the loom, when she peeped out at him with black face and hands again and said, "Eppie in de toal hole!" This total failure of the coal-hole discipline shook Silas's belief in punishment. "She'd take it all for fun," he observed, "if I didn't hurt her, and that I can't do."

So Eppie was reared without punishment, the burden of her misdeeds being borne by Father Silas. The stone hut was made a soft nest for her, lined with downy patience; and also in the world that lay beyond the stone hut, she knew nothing of frowns and denials. — GEORGE ELIOT.

From "Silas Marner."

THE BELL OF ATRI

At Atri in Abruzzo, a small town
Of ancient Roman date, but scant renown,
One of those little places that have run
Half up the hill, beneath a blazing sun,
And then sat down to rest, as if to say,
"I climb no farther upward, come what may," —
The Re Giovanni, now unknown to fame,
So many monarchs since have borne the name,
Had a great bell hung in the market place
Beneath a roof, projecting some small space,
By way of shelter from the sun and rain.
Then rode he through the streets with all his train,
And, with the blast of trumpets loud and long,
Made proclamation, that whenever wrong
Was done to any man, he should but ring
The great bell in the square, and he, the King,
Would cause the Syndic to decide thereon.
Such was the proclamation of King John.

How swift the happy days in Atri sped,
What wrongs were righted, need not here be said.
Suffice it that, as all things must decay,
The hempen rope at length was worn away,
Unraveled at the end, and, strand by strand,
Loosened and wasted in the ringer's hand,

Till one, who noted this in passing by,
Mended the rope with braids of bryony,
So that the leaves and tendrils of the vine
Hung like a votive garland at a shrine.

By chance it happened that in Atri dwelt
A knight, with spur on heel and sword in belt,
Who loved to hunt the wild boar in the woods,
Who loved his falcons with their crimson hoods,
Who loved his hounds and horses, and all sports
And prodigalities of camps and courts; —
Loved, or had loved them; for at last, grown old,
His only passion was the love of gold.
He sold his horses, sold his hawks and hounds,
Rented his vineyards and his garden grounds,
Kept but one steed, his favorite steed of all,
To starve and shiver in a naked stall,
And day by day sat brooding in his chair,
Devising plans how best to hoard and spare.

At length he said: "What is the use or need
To keep at my own cost this lazy steed,
Eating his head off in my stables here,
When rents are low and provender is dear?
Let him go feed upon the public ways;
I want him only for the holidays."
So the old steed was turned into the heat
Of the long, lonely, silent, shadeless street;

"HE CALLS FOR JUSTICE."

And wandered in suburban lanes forlorn,
Barked at by dogs, and torn by brier and thorn.

One afternoon, as in that sultry clime
It is the custom in the summer time,
With bolted doors and window shutters closed,
The inhabitants of Atri slept or dozed;
When suddenly upon their senses fell
The loud alarum of the accusing bell!
The Syndic started from his deep repose,
Turned on his couch, and listened, and then rose
And donned his robes, and with reluctant pace
Went panting forth into the market place,
Where the great bell upon its crossbeam swung
Reiterating with persistent tongue,
In half-articulate jargon, the old song: —
"Some one hath done a wrong, hath done a wrong!"
But ere he reached the belfry's light arcade
He saw, or thought he saw, beneath its shade,
No shape of human form of woman born,
But a poor steed dejected and forlorn,
Who with uplifted head and eager eye
Was tugging at the vines of bryony.
"Domeneddio!" cried the Syndic straight,
"This is the Knight of Atri's steed of state!
He calls for justice, being sore distressed,
And pleads his cause as loudly as the best."

Meanwhile from street and lane a noisy crowd
Had rolled together like a summer cloud,
And told the story of the wretched beast
In five-and-twenty different ways at least,
With much gesticulation and appeal
To heathen gods, in their excessive zeal.
The knight was called and questioned; in reply
Did not confess the fact, did not deny;
Treated the matter as a pleasant jest,
And set at naught the Syndic and the rest,
Maintaining, in an angry undertone,
That he should do what pleased him with his own.

And thereupon the Syndic gravely read
The proclamation of the King; then said:
"Pride goeth forth on horseback grand and gay,
But cometh back on foot, and begs its way;
Fame is the fragrance of heroic deeds,
Of flowers of chivalry and not of weeds!
These are familiar proverbs; but I fear
They never yet have reached your knightly ear.
What fair renown, what honor, what repute
Can come to you from starving this poor brute?
He who serves well and speaks not, merits more
Than they who clamor loudest at the door.
Therefore the law decrees that as this steed
Served you in youth, henceforth you shall take heed

To comfort his old age, and to provide
Shelter in stall, and food and field beside."

The knight withdrew abashed; the people all
Led home the steed in triumph to his stall.
The King heard and approved, and laughed in glee,
And cried aloud: "Right well it pleaseth me!
Church bells at best but ring us to the door,
But go not in to mass; my bell doth more:
It cometh into court and pleads the cause
Of creatures dumb and unknown to the laws;
And this shall make, in every Christian clime,
The Bell of Atri famous for all time."

— H. W. Longfellow.

THE MOCKING BIRD

The plumage of the mocking bird, though none of the homeliest, has nothing gaudy or brilliant in it, and had he nothing else to recommend him, would scarcely entitle him to notice; but his figure is well proportioned, and even handsome. The ease, elegance, and rapidity of his movements, the animation of his eye, and the intelligence he displays in listening, and laying up lessons from almost every species of the feathered creation within his hearing, are really surprising, and mark the peculiarity of his genius. To these qualities we may add that of a voice full, strong, and musical, and capable of almost every modulation, from the clear, mellow tones of the wood thrush to the savage screams of the bald eagle.

In measure and accent, he faithfully follows his originals. In force and sweetness of expression, he greatly improves upon them. In his native groves, mounted upon the top of a tall bush or half-grown tree, in the dawn of dewy morning, while woods are already vocal with a multitude of warblers, his admirable song rises preëminent over every competitor. The ear can listen to *his* music alone, to which that of all the others seems a mere accompaniment. Neither is this strain altogether imitative. His own native notes, which are easily distinguishable by such as are well acquainted with those of our various birds of song, are bold and full and varied, seemingly, beyond all limits. They consist of short expressions of two, three, or at the most, five or six syllables, generally interspersed with imitations, and all of them uttered with great emphasis and rapidity, and continued with ardor, for half an hour, or an hour, at a time.

His expanded wings and tail glisten with white, and the buoyant gayety of his action arrests the eye, as his song most irresistibly does the ear. He sweeps round with the most enthusiastic ecstasy; he mounts and descends, as his song swells or dies away. He bounds aloft with the celerity of an arrow, as if to recover or recall his very soul, which expired in the last elevated strain.

While thus exerting himself, a bystander, destitute of sight, would suppose that all the feathered tribes had assembled together for a trial of skill, each striving to produce his utmost effect, — so perfect are his imitations. He many times deceives the sportsman, and sends him in search of birds that perhaps are not within miles of him, but whose notes he exactly imitates. Even birds themselves are frequently imposed on by this admirable mimic, and are decoyed by the fancied call of their mates, or dive, with precipitation, into the depths of thickets, at the scream of what they suppose to be the sparrow hawk.

The mocking bird loses little of the power and energy of his song by confinement. In his domesticated state, when he begins his career of song, it is impossible to stand by uninterested. He whistles for the dog. Cæsar starts up, wags his tail, and runs to meet his master. The bird squeaks out like a hurt chicken; and the hen hurries about, with hanging wings and bristled feathers, clucking to protect her injured brood. The barking of the dog, the mewing of the cat, the creaking of a passing wheelbarrow, follow with great truth and rapidity. He repeats the tune taught him by his master, though of considerable length, fully and faithfully. He runs over the quiverings of the canary, and the clear whistling of the Virginia nightingale or redbird, with such superior execution and effect, that the mortified songsters feel their own inferiority, and become altogether silent, while he seems to triumph in their defeat, by redoubling his exertions.

This excessive fondness for variety, however, in the opinion of some, injures his song. His elevated imitations of the brown thrush are frequently interrupted by the crowing of cocks; and the warblings of the bluebird, which he exquisitely manages, are mingled with the screaming of swallows, or the cackling of hens.

Amidst the simple melody of the robin, we are suddenly surprised by the shrill reiterations of the whip-poor-will; while the notes of the killdeer, blue jay, martin, Baltimore oriole, and twenty others succeed, with such imposing reality, that we look round for the originals, and discover, with astonishment, that the sole performer, in this singular concert, is the admirable bird before us.

During this exhibition of his powers, he spreads his wings, expands his tail, and throws himself around the cage in all the ecstasy of enthusiasm, seeming not only to sing, but to dance, keeping time to the measure of his own music.

— ALEXANDER WILSON.

THE WATER OUZEL

The waterfalls of the sierra are frequented by only one bird, — the ouzel, or water thrush. He is a singularly joyous and lovable little fellow, about the size of a robin, clad in a plain waterproof suit of bluish gray, with a tinge of chocolate on his head and shoulders.

Among all the countless waterfalls I have met in the course of my exploration in the sierra, not one was found without its ouzel. No cañon is too cold for this little bird, none too lonely, provided it be rich in falling water. Find a fall or rushing rapid anywhere upon a clear stream, and there you will find an ouzel, flitting about in the spray, diving in foaming eddies; ever vigorous yet self-contained, and neither seeking nor shunning your company.

If disturbed while dipping about in the margin shallows, he either sets off with a rapid whir to some other feeding ground, or alights on some half-submerged rock out in the current, and immediately begins to nod and courtesy like a wren, turning his head from side to side, with many other odd, dainty movements.

He is the humming bird of the waters, loving rocky ripple slopes and sheets of foam as a bee loves flowers, as a lark loves sunshine and meadows.

Among all the mountain birds, none has cheered me so much in my lonely wanderings. For both in winter and in summer he sings, and cheerily. While water sings, so must he, in heat or cold, calm or storm; low in the drought of summer and the drought of winter, but never silent.

As for weather, dark days and bright days are the same to him. The voices of most song birds, however joyous, suffer a long winter eclipse, but the ouzel sings on through all the seasons and every kind of storm. No need of spring sunshine to thaw his song, for it never freezes. Never shall you hear anything wintry from his warm breast; no wavering notes between sorrow and joy. His mellow, fluty voice is ever tuned to gladness.

One cold winter morning I sallied forth to see what I might learn and enjoy. The loose snow was already over five feet deep on the meadows, but I made my way to a certain ripple on the river where one of my ouzels lived. He was at home, busily gleaning his breakfast among the pebbles, apparently unaware of anything extraordinary in the weather. Presently he flew out to a stone against which the icy current was beating, and turning his back to the wind, sang as delightfully as a lark in springtime.

I found a few sparrows busy at the feet of the larger trees gleaning seeds and insects, joined now and then by a robin. A solitary gray eagle was braving the storm on the top of a tall pine stump. He was standing bolt upright, with his back to the wind, a tuft of snow piled on his square shoulders,— a monument of passive endurance. Every snow-bound bird seemed more or less uncomfortable, if not in positive distress. Not one cheerful note came from a single bill. Their patient suffering offered a striking contrast to the spontaneous gladness of the ouzel, who could no more help exhaling sweet song than a rose sweet fragrance.

The songs of the ouzel are exceedingly difficult of description. Though I have been acquainted with my favorite ten years, and have heard him sing nearly every day, I still detect notes and strains that seem new to me. Nearly all of his music is sweet and tender, flowing from his round breast like water over the smooth lip of a pool, and then breaking into a sparkling foam of melodious notes.

The ouzel never sings in chorus with other birds, but only with the streams. I have often observed him singing in the midst of beaten spray, his music completely buried beneath the water's roar. Yet I knew he was surely singing, by his gestures and the movements of his bill.

His food consists of all kind of water insects, which in summer are chiefly found along shallow margins.

Here he wades about, ducking his head under water and deftly turning over pebbles and fallen leaves with his bill. He seldom chooses to go into deep water, where he has to use his wings in diving.

During the winter, when the streams are chilled nearly to the freezing point, so that the snow falling into them is not wholly dissolved, — then he seeks the deeper portions of the rivers where he may dive to clear water.

One stormy morning in winter when the Merced River was blue and green with unmelted snow, I observed an ouzel perched on a snag in the midst of a swift-rushing rapid. He was singing cheerily, as if everything was just to his mind. While I stood on the bank admiring him, he suddenly plunged into the current, leaving his song abruptly broken off. After feeding a minute or two at the bottom, and when one would suppose that he must surely be swept far down stream, he emerged just where he went down. Alighting on the same snag, he showered the water beads from his feathers, and continued his unfinished song.

The ouzel's nest is one of the most extraordinary pieces of bird architecture I ever saw, odd and novel in design, and in every way worthy of the genius of the little builder. It is about a foot in diameter, round in outline, with a neatly arched opening near the bottom, somewhat like an old-fashioned brick oven. It is built chiefly of the green and yellow mosses that cover the rocks and drift logs near the waterfalls. These are deftly interwoven into a charming little hut, and so situated that many of the outer mosses continue to grow as if they had not been plucked. The site chosen for the curious mansion is usually some little rock shelf within reach of the lighter spray of a waterfall, so that its walls are kept green and growing.

In these moss huts three or four eggs are laid, white, like foam bubbles. And well may the little birds hatched from them sing water songs, for they hear them all their lives. I have often observed the young just out of the nest making their odd gestures, and seeming in every way as much at home as their experienced parents. No amount of familiarity with people and their ways seems to change them in the least.

Even so far north as icy Alaska, I have found my glad singer. One cold day in November I was exploring the glaciers between Mount Fairweather and the Stikeen River. After trying in vain to force a way through the icebergs, I was weary and baffled, and sat resting in my canoe. While I thus lingered, drifting with the bergs, I suddenly heard the well-known whir of an ouzel's wings, and, looking up, saw my little comforter coming straight across the ice from the shore. In a second or two he was with me, flying around my head with a happy salute, as if to say: —

"Cheer up, old friend, you see I am here, and all's well."

Then he flew back to the shore, alighted on the topmost jag of a stranded iceberg, and began to nod and bow as though he were on one of his favorite bowlders in the midst of a sunny sierra cascade.

Such, then, is our little water ouzel, beloved of every one who is so fortunate as to know him. Tracing on strong wing every curve of the swiftest torrent, not fearing to follow it through its darkest gorges and its coldest snow tunnels; acquainted with every waterfall, he echoes its divine music.

— JOHN MUIR.

From " The Mountains of California."

THE DAFFODILS

I WANDERED lonely as a cloud
That floats on high o'er vales and hills,
When all at once I saw a crowd,
A host, of golden daffodils;
Beside the lake, beneath the trees,
Fluttering and dancing in the breeze.

Continuous as the stars that shine
And twinkle on the milky way,
They stretched in never ending line
Along the margin of the bay;
Ten thousand saw I at a glance,
Tossing their heads in sprightly dance.

The waves beside them danced; but they
Outdid the sparkling waves in glee;
A poet could not but be gay,
In such a jocund company;
I gazed — and gazed — but little thought
What wealth to me the show had brought.

For oft, when on my couch I lie
In vacant or in pensive mood,
They flash upon the inward eye,
Which is the bliss of solitude;
And then my heart with pleasure fills,
And dances with the daffodils.

— WILLIAM WORDSWORTH.

WHERE LIES THE LAND?

WHERE lies the land to which the ship would go?
Far, far ahead, is all her seamen know.
And where the land she travels from? Away,
Far, far behind, is all that they can say.

On sunny noons upon the deck's smooth face,
Linked arm in arm, how pleasant here to pace;
Or, o'er the stern reclining, watch below
The foaming wake far widening as we go.

On stormy nights when wild northwesters rave,
How proud a thing to fight with wind and wave!
The dripping sailor on the reeling mast
Exults to bear, and scorns to wish it past.

Where lies the land to which the ship would go?
Far, far ahead, is all her seamen know.
And where the land she travels from? Away,
Far, far behind, is all that they can say.
— ARTHUR HUGH CLOUGH.

THE CZAR AND THE ANGEL

SOMEWHERE, nowhere, in a certain empire, time out of mind, and in no land of ours, dwelt a Czar who was so very proud that he feared neither God nor man. He listened to no good counsel, but did only that which was good in his own eyes, and no one dared to put him right. And all his ministers and nobles grieved exceedingly, and all the people grieved likewise.

One day the Czar went to church and he listened to the priest who was reading from the Scriptures.

Now there were certain words in the holy book which pleased not the Czar. "Why say such words to me?" thought he, "words that I can never forget, though I grow gray-headed." After service the Czar went home, and bade his servants send the priest to him. The priest came.

"How darest thou to read such words to me?" asked the Czar.

"They were written to be read," replied the priest.

"Written, indeed! And wouldst thou then read everything that is written? Blot out those words and never dare to read them again, I command thee!"

"It is not I who have written the words of the Holy Scripture, your Majesty," said the priest; "nor is it for me to blot them out."

"What! thou dost presume to teach me? I am the Czar, and it is thy duty to obey me."

"In all things will I obey thee, O Czar, save only in sacred things. God is over them; men cannot alter them," answered the priest.

"Not alter them!" roared the Czar; "if I wish them altered, altered they must be. Strike me out those words instantly, I say, and never dare read them in church again. Dost thou hear?"

"I dare not," said the priest. "I have no will in the matter."

"I COMMAND THEE, FELLOW!"

"I command thee, fellow!"

"I dare not, O Czar!"

"Well," said the Czar, "I'll give thee three days to think about it. On the evening of the fourth day appear before me, and I'll strike thy head from thy shoulders if thou dost not obey me!"

Then the priest bowed low and returned to his home.

The third day was already drawing to a close and the priest knew not what to do. It was no great terror to him to die for the faith, but what would become of his wife and children? He walked about, and wept, and wrung his hands:—

"Oh, woe is me! woe is me!"

At last he lay down on his bed, but not until dawn did he close his eyes in sleep. Then he saw in a dream an angel standing at his head.

"Fear nothing!" said the angel. "God hath sent me down on earth to protect thee!"

So, early in the morning, the priest rose up full of joy and prayed gratefully to God.

The Czar also awoke early in the morning, and shouted to his huntsmen to gather together and go hunting with him in the forest.

So away they went to the hunt, and it was not long before a stag leaped out of the thicket beneath the very eyes of the Czar. He galloped after it. Every moment the stag seemed to be faltering, and yet the Czar could never quite come up with it. Eager with excitement, he spurred on his horse.

"Faster, faster!" he cried; "now we have him!"

But here a stream crossed the road, and the stag plunged into the water. The Czar was a good swimmer. "Surely I shall take him now," thought he. "A little longer, and I shall hold him by the horns."

So the Czar took off his clothes, and into the water he plunged after the stag. The stag swam across to the opposite bank, but just as the Czar was extending his hand to seize him by the horns, there was no longer any stag to be seen. It was the angel who had taken the form of a stag. The Czar was amazed. He looked about him on every side, and wondered where the stag had gone.

At that moment he saw some one on the other side of the river, putting on the Czar's royal clothes, and presently he mounted the Czar's own horse and galloped away. The Czar thought it was some evil doer, but it was the self-same angel, who had now gone away to collect the huntsmen and take them home. As for the Czar, he remained all naked and solitary in the forest.

At last he looked about him and saw, far, far away, smoke rising above the forest, and something like a dark cloud standing in the clear sky.

"Perhaps," said he to himself, " that smoke is from my hunting pavilion."

So he went in the direction of the smoke, and came at last to a brickkiln. The brick burners came forth to meet him, and were amazed to see a man without clothing. They saw that his feet were lame and bruised, and his body covered with scratches.

"Give me to drink," said he, "and I would fain eat something also."

The brick burners had pity on him; they gave him an old tattered garment to wear, and a piece of black bread to eat. Never from the day of his birth had the Czar had such a tasty meal.

"And now speak, O man!" said they; "who art thou?"

"I'll tell you who I am," said he, when he had eaten his fill; "I am your Czar. Lead me to my capital, and there I will reward you!"

"What, thou wretched rogue!" they cried. "Thou dost presume to mock us, thou old ragamuffin, and magnify thyself into a Czar! Thou reward us, indeed!"

And they looked at him in amazement and scorn.

"Dare to laugh at me again," said he, "and I'll have your heads chopped off!"

For he forgot himself, and thought he was at home.

"What! Thou!" shouted the brick burners, and

they fell upon him, and beat him most unmercifully, and then they drove him away, and off he went, groaning, into the forest.

He went on and on till at last he saw once more a smoke rising up out of the wood. Again he thought:

"That is surely from my hunting pavilion," and so he went up to it.

And behold, he had come to another brickkiln. There, too, they had pity upon and kindly treated him. They gave him to eat and to drink. They also gave him ragged hose and a tattered shirt, for they were very poor people. They took him to be a runaway soldier, or some other poor man; but when he had eaten his fill and clothed himself he said to them:—

"I am your Czar!"

They laughed at him, and again he began to talk roughly to the people. Then they fell upon him, and thrashed him soundly, and drove him away. And he wandered all by himself through the forest till it was night. Then he laid himself down beneath a tree, and slept until the morning, when he continued his journey.

At last he came to a third brickkiln, but he did not tell the brick burners there that he was the Czar. All he thought of now was how he might reach his capital. These people too, treated him kindly, and seeing that his feet were lame and bruised they had compassion upon him, and gave him a pair of very old boots. And he asked them: —

"Do ye know by which way I can get to the capital?"

They told him; but it was a long, long road and a weary journey.

But he followed the road which they had pointed out. He went on and on till he came to a little town, and there the roadside sentries stopped him.

"Halt!" they cried.

He halted.

"Whence art thou?" asked the soldiers.

"I am going to the capital," answered the Czar.

"Thou art a vagabond," they cried.

So they took him to the capital and put him in a dungeon. After a time the custodians came round to examine the prisoner.

"Who art thou, old man?" they asked. Then he told them the whole truth.

"Once I was the Czar," said he, and he related all that had befallen him. They were amazed, for he was not at all like a Czar. For indeed he had been growing thin and haggard for a long time, and his beard was all long and tangled. And yet, for all that, he insisted that he was the Czar. So they made up their minds that he was crazy, and drove him away. "Why should we keep this fool forever," said they, "and waste the Czar's bread upon him?"

Then they let him go, and never did any man feel so wretched on God's earth as did that wretched Czar. Willingly would he have done any sort of work if he had only known how, but he had never been used to work, and therefore was obliged to beg his bread, and could scarce beg enough to keep body and soul together. He lay at night at the first place that came to hand, sometimes in the tall grass, sometimes beneath a fence.

"Who could have thought that it should ever come to this!" he sighed.

Now the angel, who had made himself Czar, had gone home with the huntsmen. And no man knew that he was not a Czar but an angel. The same evening the priest came to him and said: —

"Do thy will, O Czar, and strike off my head, for I cannot blot out one word of Holy Scripture."

And the Czar said to him: —

"Glory be to God, for now I know that there is at least one priest in my land who stands firm for God's Word. I'll make thee the highest bishop in this realm."

The priest thanked him, bowed down to the earth, and departed, marveling.

"What is this wonder," thought he, "that the

haughty Czar should have become so just and gentle?"

But all men marveled at the change that had come over the ruler. He was now mild and gracious, no longer did he spend all his days in the forest, but went about inquiring of his people if any were wronged or injured by their neighbors, and if justice were done. He took count of all, and rebuked the unjust judges, and saw that every man had his rights. And the people now rejoiced as much as they had grieved heretofore, and justice was done in all the courts, and no bribes were taken. But the Czar, the real Czar, grew more and more wretched.

Then, after three years, an order went forth from the palace that all the people were to come together to a great banquet given by the Czar; all were to be there, both rich and poor, both high and lowly. And all the people came, and the unhappy Czar came too. And so many long tables were set out in the Czar's courtyard that all the people praised God when they saw the glad sight.

They all sat down at table and ate and drank, and the Czar himself and his courtiers distributed the meat and drink to the guests as much as they would, but to the unfortunate Czar they gave a double portion of everything. When all had eaten and drunk their fill, the Czar that ruled over the land began to inquire whether any had suffered injustice or wrong. And when the people began to disperse, the Czar stood at the gate and gave to every one a piece of money.

And again, after three years, he made yet another banquet, and proclaimed that all should come, both rich and poor. And all the people came and ate and drank and bowed low before the angel Czar and thanked him and made ready to depart. The unlucky Czar was also on the point of going, when the angel Czar stopped him, and took him aside into the palace, and said to him: —

"Lo! God hath tried thee and chastised thy pride these many years. But me he sent to teach thee that a Czar must have regard to the complaints of his people. So thou wast made poor and a vagabond that thou mightest pick up wisdom, if but a little. Look now, that thou doest good to thy people, and judgest righteous judgment, as now thou shalt be Czar again, but I must return to heaven." And when the angel had said this he was no more to be seen.

Then the Czar prayed gratefully to God, and from henceforth he ruled his people justly, as the angel had bidden him.

From "Cossack Fairy Tales and Folk Tales."

THE SEA VOYAGE

I was born in the East Indies. I lost my father and mother when I was very young. At the age of five, my relations thought it proper that I should be sent to England for my education. I was to be intrusted to the care of a young woman, but just as I had taken leave of my friends and we were about to take our passage, she suddenly fell sick and could not go on board.

The ship was at the very point of sailing, and it was the last that was to sail for the season. At length the captain prevailed upon my friends to let me embark alone. There was no possibility of getting any other attendant for me in the short time allotted for our preparation, and the opportunity of going by that ship was thought too valuable to be lost. No ladies happened to be going, and so I was consigned to the care of the captain and his crew, — rough and unaccustomed attendants for a young creature delicately brought up as I had been.

The unpolished sailors were my nursery mates and my waiting women. Everything was done by the captain and the men to accommodate me and make me comfortable. I had a little room made out of the cabin, which was to be considered as my room, and nobody might enter it.

The first mate had a great character for bravery and all sailorlike accomplishments; but with all this, he had a gentleness of manner, and a pale, feminine cast of face, from ill health and a weakly constitution, which subjected him to some ridicule from the officers, and caused him to be named Betsy. He did not much like the appellation; but he submitted to it, saying that those who gave him a woman's name well knew that he had a man's heart, and that in the face of danger he would go as far as any man. To this young man, whose real name was Charles Atkinson, the care of me was especially intrusted.

Betsy was proud of his charge, and, to do him justice, acquitted himself with great diligence and adroitness through the whole voyage. This reconciled me, in some measure, to the want of a maid, which I had been used to. But I was a manageable girl at all times and gave nobody much trouble.

I have not knowledge enough to give an account of my voyage, or to remember the names of the seas we passed through, or the lands which we touched upon in our course. The chief thing I can remember was Atkinson taking me up on deck to see the whales playing about in the sea. There was one great whale that came bounding up out of the sea; then he would dive into it again, and then he would come up at a distance where nobody expected him; and another whale was following after him. Atkinson said they were at play, and that the lesser whale kept the bigger whale company all through the wide seas. But I thought it frightful kind of play, for every minute I expected they would come up to our ship and toss it. But Atkinson said that a whale was a gentle creature, that it was a sort of sea elephant, and that the most powerful creatures in nature are always the least hurtful.

Many other things he used to show me when he was not on watch or doing some duty for the ship. No one was more attentive to his duty than he; but at such times as he had leisure he would show me all the pretty sea sights, — the dolphins and the porpoises that came before a storm, and all the colors which the sea changed to, — how sometimes it was a deep blue, and then a deep green, and sometimes it would seem all on fire. All these various appearances he would show me and attempt to explain the reason for them to me as well as my young capacity would admit of.

There were a lion and a tiger on board, going to England as a present to the king, and it was a great diversion for Atkinson and me to see the ways of these beasts in their dens, and how venturous the sailors were in putting their hands through the gates and patting their rough coats.

Some of the men had monkeys which ran loose about; and the sport was for the men to lose them and find them again. The monkeys would run up the shrouds and pass from rope to rope with ten times greater alacrity than the most experienced sailor could follow them. Sometimes they would hide themselves in the most unthought-of places, and when they were found they would grin and make mouths. Atkinson described to me the ways of these little animals in their native woods, for he had seen them. Oh, how many ways he thought of to amuse me in that long voyage!

Sometimes he would describe to me the odd shapes and varieties of fishes that were in the sea; and tell me tales of the sea monsters that lay hid at the bottom and were seldom seen by men; and what a curious sight it would be if our eyes could be sharpened to behold all the inhabitants of the sea at once, swimming in the great deeps, as plain as we see the gold and silver fish in a bowl of glass. With such notions he enlarged my infant capacity to take in many things.

When, in foul weather, I was terrified at the motion of the vessel, as it rocked backwards and forwards, he would still my fears and tell me that I used to be rocked so once in a cradle; and that the sea was God's bed and the ship our cradle, and we were as safe in that greater motion as when we felt that lesser one in our little wooden sleeping places. When the wind was up and sang through the sails and disturbed me with its violent clamor, he would call it music, and bid me hark to the sea organ; and with that name he quieted my tender apprehensions.

When I looked around with a mournful face, he would enter into my thoughts and tell me pretty stories of his mother and sisters, and a cousin that he loved better than his sisters, whom he called Jenny. One time, and never but once, he told me that Jenny had promised to be his wife if ever he returned to England; but that he had his doubts whether he should live to get home. This made me cry bitterly.

The captain and all were singularly kind to me and strove to make up for my uneasy and unnatural situation. The boatswain would pipe for my diversion, and the sailor boy would climb the dangerous mast for my sport. The rough foremastman would never willingly appear before me till he had combed his long black hair smooth and sleek, so as not to terrify me. The officers got up a sort of play for my amusement; and Atkinson, or, as they called him, Betsy, acted the heroine of the piece. All ways that could be contrived were thought upon to reconcile me to my lot.

I was the universal favorite; I do not know how deservedly, but I suppose it was because I was alone. Had I come over with relations or attendants, I should have excited no particular curiosity; I should have required no uncommon attentions. I was one little woman among a crew of men; and I believe the homage (which I have read) that men universally pay to women, was in this case directed to me in the absence of all other womankind. I do not know how that may be; but I was a little princess among them, and I was not six years old.

I remember the first drawback which happened to my comfort was Atkinson's not appearing the whole of one day. The captain tried to reconcile me by saying that Mr. Atkinson was confined to his cabin; that he was not quite well, but a day or two would restore him. I begged to be taken in to see him, but this was not granted.

At length, by the desire of Atkinson himself, as I have since learned, I was permitted to go into his cabin and see him. He was sitting up, apparently in a state of great exhaustion; but his face lighted up when he saw me and he kissed me, and told me that he was going a great voyage far longer than that which we had passed together, and he never should come back. And though I was so young, I understood well enough that he meant this of his death;

and I cried sadly. But he comforted me and told me that I must be his little executrix and perform his last will, and bear his last words to his mother and sisters and to his cousin Jenny, whom I should see in a short time. He gave me his blessing as a father would bless his child; and he sent a kiss by me to his mother and sisters; and he made me promise that I would go and see them when I got to England.

Soon after this, he died; but I was in another part of the ship and I was not told of his death till we got to shore a few days after. Oh, what a grief it was when I learned that I had lost an old shipmate who had made an irksome situation so bearable by his kind assiduities! And to think that he was gone, and I could never repay him for his kindness!

When I had been a year and a half in England, the captain, who had made another voyage to India and back, prevailed upon my friends to let him introduce me to Atkinson's mother and sisters. Jenny was no more: she had died in the interval, and I never saw her.

In the mother and sisters of this excellent young man I have found the most valuable friends I possess on this side of the great ocean. From them I have learned passages of his former life; and this, in particular, — that the illness of which he died was brought on by a wound which he got in a desperate attempt, when he was quite a boy, to defend his captain against a superior force. By his premature valor in spiriting the men, they finally succeeded in repulsing the enemy.

This was that Atkinson, who, from his pale and feminine appearance, was called Betsy; this was he who condescended to play the handmaid to a little, unaccompanied orphan that fortune had cast upon the care of a rough sea captain and his rougher crew.

— CHARLES LAMB.

From " Eliana."

THE LESSON OF THE FERN

In a valley, centuries ago,
   Grew a little fern leaf green and slender —
   Veining delicate and fibers tender —
Waving, when the wind crept down so low;
   Rushes tall and moss, and grass grew round it,
   Playful sunbeams darted in and found it,
   Drops of dew stole in by night and crowned it,
But no foot of man e'er trod that way;
Earth was young, and keeping holiday.

Monster fishes swam the silent main,
   Stately forests waved their giant branches,
   Mountains hurled their snowy avalanches,

Mammoth creatures stalked across the plain;
   Nature reveled in grand mysteries,
   But the little fern was not of these,
   Did not number with the hills and trees;
Only grew and waved its sweet wild way —
No one came to note it day by day.

Earth one time put on a frolic mood,
   Heaved the rocks and hanged the mighty motion
   Of the deep, strong currents of the ocean;
Moved the plain and shook the haughty wood;
   Crushed the little fern in soft, moist clay,
   Covered it, and hid it safe away;
   O, the long, long centuries since that day!
O, the agony! O, life's bitter cost,
Since that useless little fern was lost!

Useless? Lost? There came a thoughtful man,
   Searching nature's secrets, far and deep;
   From a fissure in a rocky steep
He withdrew a stone, o'er which there ran
   Fairy pencilings, a quaint design,
   Veinings, leafage, fibers, clear and fine,
   And the fern's life lay in every line!
So, I think, God hides some souls away,
Sweetly to surprise us the last day.

               — MARY L. BOLLES BRANCH.

OLIVER GOLDSMITH

"THE most beloved of English writers," — what a title that is for a man! Oliver Goldsmith, a wild youth, wayward, but full of tenderness and affection, quits the country village where his boyhood has been passed in happy musing, in fond longing to see the great world, and to achieve a name and a fortune for himself.

After years of dire struggle, of neglect and poverty, — his heart turning back as fondly to his native place as it had longed eagerly for change when sheltered there, — he writes a book and a poem, full of the recollections and feelings of home, — he paints the friends and scenes of his youth, and peoples Auburn and Wakefield with remembrances of Lissoy. Wander he must, but he carries away a home-relic with him, and dies with it on his breast.

His nature is truant; in repose, it longs for change, as, on the journey, it looks back for friends and quiet. He passes to-day in building an air castle for to-morrow, or in writing yesterday's elegy; and he would fly away this hour, but that a cage and necessity keep him. What is the charm of his verse, of his style, and humor, — his sweet regrets, his delicate compassion, his soft smile, his tremulous sympathy, the weakness which he owns? Your love for him is half pity.

You come, hot and tired, from the day's battle, and this sweet minstrel sings to you. Who could harm the kind, vagrant harper? Whom did he ever hurt? He carries no weapon, save the harp on which he plays to you, and with which he delights great and humble, young and old, the captains in the tents, or the soldiers round the fire, or the women and children in the villages, at whose porches he stops and sings his simple songs of love and beauty. With that sweet story, "The Vicar of Wakefield," he has found entry into every castle and every hamlet in Europe. Not one of us, however busy or hard, but, once or twice in our lives, has passed an evening with him, and undergone the charm of his delightful music.

Think of him, reckless, thriftless, vain — if you like — but merciful, gentle, generous, full of love and pity. Think of the wonderful and unanimous response of affection with which the world has paid back the love he gave it. His humor delights us still; his song is fresh and beautiful as when first he charmed with it; his very weaknesses are beloved and familiar, — his benevolent spirit seems still to smile upon us, to do gentle kindnesses, to succor with sweet charity, to soothe, caress, and forgive; to plead with the fortunate for the unhappy and the poor. — W. M. THACKERAY.

THE VILLAGE OF AUBURN

   Sweet Auburn! loveliest village of the plain,
Where health and plenty cheered the laboring swain;
Where smiling spring its earliest visit paid,
And parting summer's lingering blooms delayed;
Dear lovely bowers of innocence and ease,
Seats of my youth, when every sport could please;
How often have I loitered o'er thy green,
Where humble happiness endeared each scene!
How often have I paused on every charm!
The sheltered cot, the cultivated farm,
The never-failing brook, the busy mill,
The decent church that topped the neighboring hill,
The hawthorn bush, with seats beneath the shade,
For talking age and whispering lovers made!

   How often have I blessed the coming day,
When toil remitting lent its turn to play!
And all the village train, from labor free,
Led up their sports beneath the spreading tree;
While many a pastime circled in the shade,
The young contending as the old surveyed;
And many a gambol frolicked o'er the ground,
And sleights of art and feats of strength went round
And still, as each repeated pleasure tired,
Succeeding sports the mirthful band inspired:

The dancing pair that simply sought renown,
By holding out to tire each other down;
The swain, mistrustless of his smutted face,
While secret laughter tittered round the place;
The bashful virgin's sidelong looks of love,
The matron's glance that would those looks reprove —
These were thy charms, sweet village! sports like these,
With sweet succession, taught e'en toil to please.

— Oliver Goldsmith.

THE VILLAGE PREACHER

Near yonder copse, where once the garden smiled,
And still where many a garden flower grows wild,
There, where a few torn shrubs the place disclose,
The village preacher's modest mansion rose.

A man he was to all the country dear,
And passing rich with forty pounds a year;
Remote from towns, he ran his godly race,
Nor e'er had changed, nor wished to change, his place.

Unskillful he to fawn, or seek for power,
By doctrines fashioned to the varying hour;
Far other aims his heart had learned to prize, —
More bent to raise the wretched than to rise.

His house was known to all the vagrant train;
He chid their wand'rings, but relieved their pain.
The long-remembered beggar was his guest,
Whose beard, descending, swept his aged breast;
The ruined spendthrift, now no longer proud,
Claimed kindred there, and had his claims allowed;

The broken soldier, kindly bade to stay,
Sat by his fire, and talked the night away, —
Wept o'er his wounds, or, tales of sorrow done,
Shouldered his crutch and showed how fields were
 won!

Pleased with his guests, the good man learned to glow,
And quite forgot their vices in their woe;
Careless their merits or their faults to scan,
His pity gave, ere charity began.

Thus to relieve the wretched was his pride,
And even his failings leaned to virtue's side;
But in his duty prompt at every call,
He watched and wept, he prayed and felt for all:

And as a bird each fond endearment tries,
To tempt her new-fledged offspring to the skies,
He tried each art, reproved each dull delay,
Allured to brighter worlds, and led the way.

Beside the bed where parting life was laid,
And sorrow, guilt, and pain by turns dismayed,
The reverend champion stood. At his control,
Despair and anguish fled the struggling soul;
Comfort came down the trembling wretch to raise,
And his last faltering accents whispered praise.

At church, with meek and unaffected grace,
His looks adorned the venerable place;
Truth from his lips prevailed with double sway;
And fools, who came to scoff, remained to pray.

The service past, around the pious man,
With ready zeal, each honest rustic ran;
Even children followed with endearing wile,
And plucked his gown, to share the good man's smile;

His ready smile a parent's warmth expressed;
Their welfare pleased him, and their cares distressed;
To them his heart, his love, his griefs were given,
But all his serious thoughts had rest in Heaven;

As some tall cliff, that lifts its awful form,
Swells from the vale, and midway leaves the storm,
Though round its breast the rolling clouds are spread,
Eternal sunshine settles on its head.

—Oliver Goldsmith.

THE VILLAGE SCHOOLMASTER

Beside yon straggling fence that skirts the way,
With blossomed furze unprofitably gay,
There, in his noisy mansion, skilled to rule,
The village master taught his little school —
A man severe he was, and stern to view;
I knew him well, and every truant knew.
Well had the boding tremblers learned to trace
The day's disasters in his morning face;
Full well they laughed with counterfeited glee
At all his jokes, for many a joke had he;
Full well the busy whisper, circling round,
Conveyed the dismal tidings when he frowned.

Yet he was kind; or, if severe in aught,
The love he bore to learning was in fault;
The village all declared how much he knew;
'Twas certain he could write, and cipher too;
Lands he could measure, terms and tides presage,
And even the story ran that he could gauge;
In arguing, too, the parson owned his skill,
For, e'en though vanquished, he could argue still;
While words of learnèd length and thundering sound
Amazed the gazing rustics ranged around;
And still they gazed, and still the wonder grew,
That one small head could carry all he knew.

But past is all his fame: the very spot
Where many a time he triumphed is forgot.

— OLIVER GOLDSMITH.

A GREAT PHILOSOPHER

SOCRATES was of humble birth. He was born in Greece nearly five hundred years before Christ, and lived for seventy years. His father was a sculptor, and he followed the same profession.

We know very little about the events of his life except that he served as a soldier in three campaigns, that he strictly obeyed the laws of his country, and once when acting as a judge refused at the peril of his life to perform an unjust deed.

A striking picture is given us of the personal appearance of this great philosopher. His ugliness of face was a matter of jest in Athens. He had a flat nose, thick lips, and prominent eyes. Yet he was as strong as he was ugly. Few Athenians could equal him in strength and endurance. While serving as a soldier he was able to bear heat and cold, hunger and fatigue in a manner that astonished his companions. He went barefoot in all weather, and wore the same clothing winter and summer. He lived on the simplest food, and it was his constant aim to limit his wants, and to avoid all excesses.

SOCRATES TAKING LEAVE OF HIS DISCIPLES.

Socrates possessed the highest and noblest qualities of mind. Naturally he had a violent temper, but he held it under severe control. In depth of thought, and in powers of argument, he stands in the very first ranks of the teachers of mankind.

From morning till night Socrates might be seen in the streets and public places engaged in endless talk, — prattling, his enemies called it. In the early morning his pale face and his sturdy figure, shabbily dressed, were familiar visions in the public walks and in the Athenian schools. At the hour when the market place was most crowded Socrates would be there, walking about among the booths and tables, and talking to every one that would listen to him. Thus was his whole day spent. He was ready to talk with any one, old or young, rich or poor.

None seemed to tire of hearing this wise man, and many sought him in his haunts eager to learn from him. Many, indeed, came from other cities of Greece, drawn to Athens by his fame, and anxious to hear the wonderful teacher. These became known as his scholars or disciples, though he had nothing like a school, and received no pay for his teaching.

The talk of Socrates was never idle nor meaningless chat. He felt that he had a special mission to fulfill, and he declared that a divine voice spoke to him and kept him from unwise acts or sayings. It had been said that no man was wiser than Socrates. To find out if this was true he questioned everybody everywhere, seeking to learn what other men knew. Leading them on by question after question he usually found that they knew very little.

But his keen questions which exposed the ignorance of so many did not make him friends. In truth he made many enemies. All this went on until some of them made the charge that he did not believe in the gods of Athens, and that he misled young men. "The penalty due for these crimes," they said, " is death."

Socrates had now so many enemies that the accusation was dangerous. When brought before the council the philosopher pleaded his own cause, but in his defense he made his case worse. He said things that provoked his judges.

"There is one true God," he declared, "who governs the world, and sends me the inward voice which tells me the way in which I should walk. This divine voice I try to obey to the utmost of my power. Because I am thought to have some ability in teaching youth, O my judges! is that a reason why I should suffer death? You may decree that my body must die, but hurt *me* you cannot." Thus he ended his defense.

Socrates did not seem to care what verdict his

judges brought. He had no fear of death and would not trouble himself to say a word to preserve his life. The voice within him would not permit him to do so. He was sentenced to drink the poison of hemlock, and was imprisoned for thirty days, during which time he conversed in his old, calm manner with his friends.

Some of his disciples planned for his escape, but he refused to fly. If his fellow-citizens wished to take his life, he would not oppose their wills. One of his friends began to weep at the thought of his dying innocent. "What!" he said, "would you think it better for me to die guilty?"

On the last day he drank the hemlock as calmly as though it were his usual beverage, and talked on quietly until death sealed his lips. Thus died the first and one of the greatest of moral philosophers, and a man without a parallel in all the history of mankind.

"Of all we have ever known," said his famous pupil Plato, "Socrates was in death the noblest,— in life the wisest and best."

— CHARLES MORRIS.

From " Historical Tales."

THE STORY OF LAFAYETTE

I. HIS BOYHOOD

The château of Chavaniac was in the province of Auvergne, in the south part of France. It was a lofty castle, with towers and narrow windows from which cannon once frowned down upon besieging foes. There was a deep moat around it, with a bridge which was drawn up in time of war, so that no man, on horseback or on foot, could pass in at the gate without permission of the guard.

Low hills, crowned with vineyards, stood near the castle, and beyond the hills stretched mountains whose peaks seemed to pierce the sky. In all France there was not a more charming spot than Chavaniac; and among all the nobles of the court there was no braver man than its master, the Marquis de Lafayette.

One day the drawbridge was let down over the moat, and the gallant marquis rode away to the war in Germany. After taking part in several engagements, he was shot through the heart in a skirmish at Minden. His comrades buried him on the field. The drums were muffled, the band played a funeral dirge, and three rounds of musketry announced that the hero's body had been lowered into the grave.

In the midst of the mourning for the dead marquis, on September 6, 1757, his only son was born.

The little orphan, according to the custom in France, received a long name at his christening, but his loving mother said that his everyday name should be Gilbert de Lafayette.

When Gilbert was old enough, his mother walked with him instead of leaving him to the care of servants. Sometimes they climbed a high hill to see the sun set over the towers of the château. Then she told him how the De Lafayettes, long before Columbus discovered America, had helped to banish the English kings from France, and how his own father had died for the glory of his country.

Sometimes as they walked through the halls of the castle, she showed Gilbert the coats of mail which his ancestors had worn; and she told him about the swords and banners and other trophies which the De Lafayettes had won in battle.

"I would not have you less brave than they, my son," she would say.

The boy longed for the time to come when he might show his mother how very brave he was. He grew tall and strong, and carried himself like a prince. He wanted to be worthy of his great ancestors.

The year he was eight there was much excitement about a wolf which prowled in the forest, killing the sheep in the pastures and frightening the peasants nearly out of their wits. Gilbert made this wolf the object of all his walks. He would persuade his mother to sit in some shady spot while he should go a little way into the forest.

"I will return in an instant, dear mother," he always said; and, lest he might alarm her, he walked quite slowly until a turn in the road hid him from view. Then he marched quickly into the dark wood.

He did this for many days, seeing only frisking squirrels and harmless rabbits. But one morning, as he sped along a narrow path, his eyes wide open and his ears alert to catch every sound, he heard a cracking in the underbrush.

The wolf was coming! He was sure of it. His mind was made up in an instant. He would spring forward quicker than lightning and blind it with his coat, while with his arms he would choke it to death.

"It will struggle hard," he thought. "Its feet will scratch me, but I shall not mind; and when all is over I shall drag it to the feet of my mother. Then she will know, and the peasants will know, that I can rid the country of these pests."

He stood listening. His breath came fast. Again he heard the breaking of the bushes. "I ought first to surprise the beast by coming upon it quickly," he whispered.

He tore off his coat and held it firmly as he hurried on. Soon he saw the shaggy hide, and the great eyes shining through the thicket. He leaped forward with outstretched coat, and — what do you think? — he clasped in his arms a calf that had strayed from the barnyard!

It was a rude disappointment for the boy. He returned to his mother, who was already alarmed at his absence, and confessed that he had tried to kill the wolf, but had found only a calf.

"Ah, you were brave, my son," she cried; "I am quite sure that you would have ended the days of that terrible wolf had he but given you the chance."

II. LAFAYETTE AND AMERICA

The young Marquis de Lafayette was a born soldier. He loved to hear the boom of cannon and the rattle of muskets on the drill ground. When he was just nineteen years old he became a captain of an artillery company.

But he said to himself, "Kings make war for conquest. I wish that I might enlist and serve for a more worthy object."

That same year an English nobleman, the royal Duke of Gloucester, chanced to visit France. He had displeased his brother, King George III, and for that reason had been banished from England.

Lafayette attended a dinner party given in honor of the royal guest. While they sat about the table, eating and drinking, a guard announced that a messenger was at the door with dispatches for his royal Highness.

"Ah, news from England!" exclaimed the duke.

"Show the man in," ordered the officer in command.

A courier, with dust on his garments, entered the room, and, bowing low, delivered a bundle of letters.

"I beg your Highness to read without ceremony," said the commander.

The duke glanced over the papers for some time in silence. He looked grave. At last he said, "My courier has brought dispatches about our colonies in America."

"Ah," said one, "are the colonies acting badly?"

"Yes, they demand to vote their own taxes."

"How absurd! Why, the people in France do not vote their own taxes."

"You must know," said the duke, "that many years ago one of the kings of England gave a charter to our people which granted them the right to impose their own taxes. They now elect representatives to a parliament, where they decide how much money should be used by the government."

"What do these Americans complain of, then?" asked Lafayette.

"Taxation without representation," answered the

duke. "They insist that, as loyal subjects, they should be allowed either to send representatives to our parliament, or have a parliament of their own. Neither privilege has been granted. Our parliament imposes taxes on them, and when they refuse to pay the taxes the king sends soldiers to force them to do so. These dispatches inform me that the rebels have driven our troops out of a town called Boston, and that delegates from the thirteen colonies have met at another town called Philadelphia and adopted a declaration of independence." After a pause, the duke added, "I am not so sure, gentlemen, but the Americans are in the right. They are fighting as freeborn Englishmen."

"The Americans *are* in the right," said Lafayette to himself; and, while the other officers were making merry, he was silent. As soon as he could do so, he excused himself from the table. He hastened to his room and locked the door.

"This is, indeed, the hour I have sought," he murmured.

He sat down to think. Presently he arose and paced the floor until it was almost morning. When, at last, he threw himself on the bed to sleep, he had resolved to leave the pleasures of rank and fortune, that he might use his sword in the defense of liberty.

About this time the American Congress sent Silas

THE SURRENDER OF CORNWALLIS. (See p. 152.)

Deane to France to seek aid; and Lafayette asked Baron de Kalb to go with him to visit the envoy.

De Kalb, who could speak both English and French, told Silas Deane that the Marquis de Lafayette wished to join the American army.

"We have no money to pay our officers," said Deane.

"I will serve without money," repeated De Kalb after Lafayette.

"We have no ship to carry you or your men," said Deane.

"I will buy a ship," was the answer.

Still the American hesitated to accept the services of such a boyish-looking officer.

But in the end Silas Deane gave Lafayette a contract to sign, in which Lafayette promised to serve in the army of the United States whenever he was wanted.

When the venerable Benjamin Franklin came to Paris, Lafayette was the first to greet him. He was enchanted with the famous philosopher, whose simple manners and plain dress befitted well the herald of a republic.

"Now, indeed, is our time of need," said Franklin.

Lafayette waited to hear no more. He bought a ship and ordered it to be equipped.

The voyage across the ocean was stormy and long.

Lafayette spent most of the time trying to learn to speak English.

His good ship *Victory* cast anchor near Charleston, South Carolina, and the party landed about midnight.

They found shelter at a farmhouse, and, on the following day, proceeded to Charleston. There Lafayette purchased carriages and horses to ride nine hundred miles to Philadelphia, where the Continental Congress was in session. When the carriages broke down because of the bad roads, the officers mounted the horses and continued their journey.

"I am more determined than ever," he said to De Kalb, "to help these people preserve the liberties they have enjoyed."

He reached Philadelphia on July 27, 1777.

III. LAFAYETTE AND WASHINGTON

When Lafayette first met Washington he knew him at once by his noble face. Washington invited the young Frenchman to cross the Delaware to see his army. When Lafayette arrived at the camp in New Jersey the troops were on the drill ground. Many of them were ragged and barefooted. Even the officers lacked suitable uniforms, and the guns were of all shapes and sizes.

"We should be embarrassed at thus showing ourselves to a French officer," said Washington.

"Ah!" replied Lafayette, with tears in his eyes; "men who fight for liberty against such odds will be sure to win."

Washington was so pleased with the modest zeal of the young marquis that he made him one of his aides.

General Howe sailed up Chesapeake Bay, and landing, marched to attack Philadelphia. Washington, with his army, went to meet him, and there was a terrible battle near Brandywine Creek.

Lafayette was in the thickest of the fight until he was forced to fall back, on account of having received a musket ball in the calf of his leg.

"Take care of the marquis as though he were my own son," said Washington to the surgeon.

The wound confined Lafayette to his bed for six weeks. When he was again able to mount a horse, he led an expedition against a post of the Hessians with such skill that he was given command of the Virginia militia.

After some battles around Philadelphia, Washington made his winter quarters at Valley Forge, about twenty miles away.

This was in the winter of 1777. The weather was very severe. Some of the soldiers were without shoes, and their feet bled as they walked over the frozen ground; yet, all through the stormy days, the little army drilled and worked at the fortifications, while at night, those without blankets sat around the camp fires to keep from freezing to death. Lafayette, who had been used to luxuries all his life, willingly shared these hardships, and went limping about from tent to tent with a pleasant word for everybody.

Now, all this time, Benjamin Franklin was at Paris, working for the colonies. But he almost despaired of securing aid from France. One day, as he sat alone wondering what plan he must next pursue, an American courier arrived from Boston. Franklin met him at the door.

"Sir," he asked, without waiting for the man to speak, "is Philadelphia captured?"

"It is, sir," answered the courier. Franklin turned sadly away. All seemed lost.

"But, sir, I have better news!" exclaimed the courier, and he showed dispatches from Congress which told of the battle of Saratoga and of Burgoyne's surrender.

Franklin was overjoyed, and hastened to court with the news.

"Really," said the king to himself, "this is the time to give John Bull a fine dose of bitters; these rebels may yet become a great nation." And so he acknowledged the independence of the United States.

Time passed, and at length all Europe was awaiting events on two rivers in America. The Hudson, in the north, lay between Clinton and Washington; in the south, the James held on its banks the opposing armies of Cornwallis and Lafayette.

Cornwallis threw up fortifications at Yorktown and moved his camp there.

Soon the French fleet moved up Chesapeake Bay and anchored before Yorktown. Lafayette marched nearer and nearer, until Cornwallis was surrounded by land and sea.

Lafayette was urged to make the attack at once. It was a temptation for the young major-general. But when he thought of the patient commander in the north, who had borne the burdens of the long war, he said: "No; I shall await the arrival of Washington. To him alone should belong the honor of giving Cornwallis this final blow."

Meanwhile, Washington left the Hudson, and when the united armies, under his command, stood in front of Yorktown, Lafayette's division was the first to storm the redoubts.

Cornwallis surrendered October 19, 1781. This ended the war, and America was free.

Lafayette returned to France. Honors were showered upon the hero, but he modestly declared that the credit of the victory belonged to Washington.

— ALMA HOLMAN BURTON.

From " Lafayette, the Friend of American Liberty."

THE AMERICAN FLAG

When Freedom, from her mountain height,
   Unfurled her standard to the air,
She tore the azure robe of night,
   And set the stars of glory there;
She mingled with its gorgeous dyes
The milky baldric of the skies,
And striped its pure celestial white
With streakings of the morning light;
Then, from his mansion in the sun,
She called her eagle bearer down,
And gave into his mighty hand
The symbol of her chosen land. . . .
Flag of the brave! thy folds shall fly,
The sign of hope and triumph, high,
When speaks the signal trumpet tone,
And the long line comes gleaming on;
Ere yet the lifeblood, warm and wet,
Has dimmed the glistening bayonet,
Each soldier eye shall brightly turn
To where thy sky-born glories burn,
And, as his springing steps advance,
Catch war and vengeance from the glance.
And when the cannon mouthings loud
Heave in wild wreaths the battle shroud,
And gory sabers rise and fall
Like shoots of flame on midnight's pall,—

Then shall thy meteor glances glow,
    And cowering foes shall sink beneath
Each gallant arm that strikes below
    That lovely messenger of death. . . .
Flag of the free heart's hope and home,
    By angel hands to valor given,
Thy stars have lit the welkin dome,
    And all thy hues were born in heaven.
Forever float that standard sheet!
    Where breathes the foe but falls before us,
With Freedom's soil beneath our feet,
    And Freedom's banner streaming o'er us?

—J. RODMAN DRAKE.

LIBERTY AND UNION

I PROFESS, sir, in my career hitherto, to have kept steadily in view the prosperity and the honor of the whole country, and the preservation of the Federal Union. I have not allowed myself to look beyond the Union, to see what might lie hidden in the dark recess behind; I have not coolly weighed the chances of preserving liberty, when the bonds that unite us together shall be broken asunder.

I have not accustomed myself to hang over the precipice of disunion, to see whether, with my short sight, I can fathom the depths of the abyss below;

nor could I regard him as a safe counselor in the affairs of this government, whose thoughts should be mainly bent on considering, not how the Union should be preserved, but how tolerable might be the condition of the poeple when it shall be broken up and destroyed.

While the Union lasts we have high, exciting, gratifying prospects spread out before us, for us and our children. Beyond that, I seek not to penetrate the veil. God grant that in my day, at least, that curtain may not rise! God grant that on my vision never may be opened what lies behind!

When my eyes shall be turned to behold, for the last time, the sun in heaven, may I not see him shining on the broken and dishonored fragments of a once glorious Union; on States dissevered, discordant, belligerent; on a land rent with civil feuds or, drenched, it may be, in fraternal blood. Let their last feeble and lingering glance rather behold the gorgeous ensign of the Republic, now known and honored throughout the earth, still full high advanced, its arms and trophies streaming in their original luster, not a stripe erased or polluted, nor a single star obscured; bearing for its motto no such miserable interrogatory as, "What is all this worth?" nor those other words of delusion and folly, "Liberty first, and Union afterwards"; but everywhere spread all over in characters of living light, blazing on all its ample folds as they float over the sea, and over the land, and in every wind under the whole heavens, that other sentiment, dear to every true American heart, "Liberty and Union, now and for ever, one and inseparable."

— Daniel Webster.

PATRIOTISM

Right and wrong, justice and crime, exist independently of our country. A public wrong is not a private right for any citizen. The citizen is a man bound to know and do the right, and the nation is but an aggregation of citizens. If a man should shout, "My country, by whatever means extended and bounded; my country, right or wrong!" he merely repeats the words of the thief who steals in the street, or of the trader who swears falsely at the customhouse, both of them chuckling, "My fortune, however acquired."

Thus, we see that a man's country is not a certain area of land, — of mountains, rivers, and woods, — but it is principle; and patriotism is loyalty to that principle.

In poetic minds and in popular enthusiasm, this feeling becomes closely associated with the soil and symbols of the country. But the secret sanctification of the soil and the symbol is the idea which they represent; and this idea the patriot worships through the name and the symbol, as a lover kisses with rapture the glove of his mistress and wears a lock of her hair upon his heart.

So, with passionate heroism, of which tradition is never weary of tenderly telling, Arnold von Winkelried gathers into his bosom the sheaf of foreign spears, that his death may give life to his country. So Nathan Hale, disdaining no service that his country demands, perishes untimely, with no other friend than God and the satisfied sense of duty. So George Washington, at once comprehending the scope of the destiny to which his country was devoted, with one hand puts aside the crown, and with the other sets his slaves free.

So, through all history from the beginning, a noble army of martyrs has fought fiercely and fallen bravely for that unseen mistress, their country. So, through all history to the end, as long as men believe in God, that army must still march and fight and fall, — recruited only from the flower of mankind, cheered only by their own hope of humanity, strong only in their confidence in their cause.

— GEORGE WILLIAM CURTIS.

WHAT MAKES A NATION?

What makes a nation? Bounding lines that lead
    from shore to shore,
That trace its girth on silent hills or on the prairie
    floor,
That hold the rivers and the lakes and all the fields
    between —
The lines that stand about the land a barrier unseen?

Or is it guns that hold the coast, or ships that sweep
    the seas,
The flag that flaunts its glory in the racing of the
    breeze;
The chants of peace, or battle hymn, or dirge, or
    victor's song,
Or parchment screed, or storied deed, that makes a
    nation strong?

What makes a nation? Is it ships or states or flags
    or guns?
Or is it that great common heart which beats in all
    her sons —
That deeper faith, that truer faith, the trust in one
    for all
Which sets the goal for every soul that hears his
    country's call?

This makes a nation great and strong and certain to
   endure,
This subtle inner voice that thrills a man and makes
   him sure,
Which makes him know there is no north or south or
   east or west
But that his land must ever stand the bravest and
   the best.
— W. D. Nesbit.

THE CHEERFUL LOCKSMITH

From the workshop of the Golden Key there issued forth a tinkling sound, so merry and good-humored, that it suggested the idea of some one working blithely, and made quite pleasant music. Tink, tink, tink — clear as a silver bell, and audible at every pause of the streets' harsher noises, as though it said, " I don't care; nothing puts me out; I am resolved to be happy."

Women scolded, children squalled, heavy carts went rumbling by, horrible cries proceeded from the lungs of hawkers; still it struck in again, no higher, no lower, no louder, no softer; not thrusting itself on people's notice a bit the more for having been outdone by louder sounds — tink, tink, tink, tink, tink.

It was a perfect embodiment of the still small voice, free from all cold, hoarseness, huskiness, or unhealthiness of any kind. Foot passengers slackened their pace, and were disposed to linger near it; neighbors who had got up splenetic that morning, felt good humor stealing on them as they heard it, and by degrees became quite sprightly; mothers danced their babies to its ringing; — still the same magical tink, tink, tink came gayly from the workshop of the Golden Key.

Who but the locksmith could have made such music? A gleam of sun shining through the unsashed window and checkering the dark workshop with a broad patch of light, fell full upon him, as though attracted by his sunny heart. There he stood working at his anvil, his face radiant with exercise and gladness, his sleeves turned up, his wig pushed off his shining forehead — the easiest, freest, happiest man in all the world.

Beside him sat a sleek cat, purring and winking in the light and falling every now and then into an idle doze, as from excess of comfort. The very locks that hung around had something jovial in their rust, and seemed like gouty gentlemen of hearty natures, disposed to joke on their infirmities.

There was nothing surly or severe in the whole scene. It seemed impossible that any one of the innumerable keys could fit a churlish strong box or a prison door. Storehouses of good things, rooms where there were fires, books, gossip, and cheering laughter — these were their proper sphere of action. Places of distrust and cruelty and restraint, they would have quadruple locked forever.

Tink, tink, tink. No man who hammered on at a dull, monotonous duty could have brought such cheerful notes from steel and iron; none but a chirping, healthy, honest-hearted fellow, who made the best of everything and felt kindly toward everybody, could have done it for an instant. He might have been a coppersmith, and still been musical. If he had sat in a jolting wagon, full of rods of iron, it seemed as if he would have brought some harmony out of it. — CHARLES DICKENS.

From "*Barnaby Rudge.*"

THE LOST CHILD. AN AUSTRALIAN STORY

Four or five miles up the river from Garoopna stood a lonely hut sheltered by a lofty bare knoll, round which the great river chafed among the bowlders. Across the stream was the forest, sloping down in pleasant glades from the mountain. Behind the hut rose a plain four or five hundred feet overhead, seeming to be held aloft by the blue stone columns which rose from the river side.

In this hut lived a shepherd and his wife and

one little boy, their son, about eight years old — a strange, wild little bush child, without any knowledge of the world, and without acquaintance with any human beings save his father and mother. He was unable to read a line; he had never received any religious training of any sort or kind. He was, in fact, as entire a little savage as you could find, and yet he was beautiful to look upon; he was as active as a wild deer, and as fearless as a lion.

As yet too young to begin labor, all the long summer days he would wander about the river bank, up and down the beautiful rock-walled paradise between the water's edge and the high level plain. Sometimes he looked eagerly across the water at the waving forest boughs, and fancied that he could see other children beckoning to him to cross and play in that merry land of shifting lights and shadows.

It grew quite into a passion with the little man to get across and play there, and one day when his mother was busy with her work he said to her: —

"Mother, what country is that across the river?"

"The forest, my child."

"There are plenty of wild flowers and ripe raspberries over there, are there not, mother? Why may I not go across and play there?"

"The river is too deep, child, and an ugly elf lives in the water under the stones."

"Who are the children that play across there?"

"Black children, likely."

"No white children?"

"No, none but pixies. Don't go near them; they will lure you on and on, nobody knows where. Don't try to cross the river or you will be drowned."

But next day the longing was stronger with him than ever. Quite early on the glorious, cloudless, midsummer day, he was down by the river side, sitting on a rock, with his shoes and stockings off, paddling his feet in the clear, tepid water, and watching the millions of little fish in the shallows, leaping and flashing in the sunlight.

There is no pleasure like a child's midsummer holiday. There sat our little boy, barelegged, watching the forbidden ground beyond the river. He sat so still that a red kingfisher perched quite close, and dashing into the water came forth with a fish, and fled like a ray of light along the winding river. A colony of little parrots, too, crowded on a bough and twittered, and ran to and fro, as though they said to him, "We don't mind you, my dear, you are one of us."

Never had the river been so low. He stepped in; it scarcely reached his ankle. Now, surely, he might get across. He stripped himself, and, carrying his clothes, waded through,—the water never reaching his waist, — all across the long, yellow, gravelly shallow. And there he stood, naked and free, on the forbidden ground.

He quickly dressed himself and began to examine his new kingdom. He found it rich far beyond his utmost hopes. Such wild flowers and such raspberries — far surpassing all that he had dreamed of. And when he had grown tired of them, such fern boughs, six or eight feet long!

He would explore this region and see how far it extended. What tales he would have for his father to-night! He would bring him here, and show him all the wonders, and perhaps his father would build a new hut over here, and come and live in it.

There! There is one of those children he had seen before across the river. Ah! Ah! it is not a child at all, but a pretty gray beast with big ears. A kangaroo, my lad; he will not play with you, but skips away slowly, and leaves you alone.

There is something like the gleam of water on that rock. A snake! Now a sounding rush through the wood, and a passing shadow. An eagle! He brushes so close to the child that he strikes at the bird with a stick, and then watches him as he shoots up like a rocket, and, measuring the fields of air in ever-widening circles, hangs like a motionless speck upon the sky.

Here is a prize, though! A wee young native bear, hardly a foot long, — an odd-looking little gray beast with broad flapping ears, — sits on a tree within easy reach. It is not afraid, but cuddles into the child's bosom, and eats a leaf as they go along. The mother sits aloft and goes on with her dinner of peppermint leaves.

What a short day it has been! Here is the sun getting low, and the birds are already going to roost. The boy would turn and go back to the river. Alas! which way?

He was lost in the forest. He turned back, and went, as he thought, the way he had come, but soon arrived at a tall cliff, which by some magic seemed to have got between him and the river. Then he broke down, and that strange madness came on him which comes even on strong men when lost in the forest — a despair, a confusion of intellect, which has cost many a man his life. Think what it must have been with this child!

He felt sure that the cliff was between him and his home. He must climb it. Alas! every step he took carried him farther and farther from the river and the hope of safety; and when he came to the top, just at dark, he saw nothing but cliff after cliff, range after range, all around him.

He had been wandering through deep gullies all

day without knowing it, and had now gone far into
the mountains. Night was coming down, still and
crystal clear, and the poor lad was far away from
help or hope, going his last long journey alone.
Partly perhaps walking, and partly sitting down and
weeping, he got through the night. And when the
solemn morning came up again he was still tottering
along, and crying from time to time, "Mother,
mother!" — still nursing his little bear, his only
companion, to his bosom, and still holding in his hand
a few poor flowers he had gathered the day before.

Up and on all day; and at evening, passing out
of the great zone of timber, he came on the bald
summit ridge where one ruined tree held up its
skeleton arms against the sunset, and the wind came
keen and frosty. So, with failing, feeble legs, he toiled
upward still, toward the region of rock and snow,
toward the lofty home of the kite and the eagle.

Brisk as they were all at Garoopna, none were so
brisk as Cecil and Samuel. Long before any others
were ready these two had strapped their blankets to
their saddles, and followed by Samuel's dog, Rover,
were cantering off up the river.

Neither spoke at first. They knew what a sad
task they had before them; and while acting as
though everything depended upon speed they guessed

well that their search would be of little help to the poor child. Still they hurried onward.

Cecil began: "Samuel, depend on it that child has crossed the river. If he had been on the plains he would have been seen from a distance in a few hours."

"I agree with you," said Samuel. "Let us go down on this side till we are opposite the hut and search for marks by the river side."

In half an hour they were opposite the hut, and, riding across to it to ask a few questions, they found the poor mother sitting on the doorstep, with her apron over her head, rocking herself to and fro.

"We have come to help you," said Cecil. "Where do you think he is gone?"

The mother answered, with frequent bursts of grief, that some days before he had spoken of seeing white children across the water who beckoned him to cross and play; that she, knowing well they were fairies, or perhaps worse, had warned him solemnly not to mind them; but that she had little doubt that they had helped him over and carried him away to the forest.

"Why, it is not knee deep across the shallow," said Cecil. "Let us cross again. He may be drowned, but I don't think so."

In a quarter of an hour from starting they found, a

little way up the stream, one of the child's stockings, which in his hurry to dress he had forgotten. Here brave Rover took up the trail like a bloodhound, and before evening stopped at the foot of a lofty cliff.

"Can he have gone up here?" said Samuel, as they gazed up the steep side of the rock.

"Most likely," answered Cecil. "Lost children always climb from height to height. I have heard this often from old woodsmen. Why they do so, God only knows; but the fact is beyond denial. Ask Rover what he thinks?"

The brave old dog was half way up, looking back for them. It took them until nearly dark to get their horses up; and as there was no moon, and the way was full of danger, they determined to camp for the night, and start again in the morning.

At early dawn they caught the horses and started afresh. Both were more silent than ever, and the dog, with his nose to the ground, led them slowly along the rocky ridge of the mountain, ever going higher and higher.

"I cannot believe," said Samuel, "that the poor child has come up here. Don't you think we must be mistaken?"

"The dog does not agree with you," said Cecil. "He has something before him not very far off. Watch him."

The trees had become small and scattered. The real forest was now below them. A few hundred yards before them they saw a dead tree, on the highest branch of which sat an eagle.

"The dog has stopped," said Cecil. "The end is near."

"See," said Samuel, "there is a handkerchief under the tree."

"That is the boy himself," said Cecil.

They were up to him and off their horses in a moment. There the poor boy lay dead and stiff, one hand still grasping the flowers he had gathered on his last happy playday, and the other laid as a pillow between the soft cold cheek and the rough cold stone. His midsummer holiday was over, his long journey ended.

— Henry Kingsley.

DUTY

One by one the sands are flowing,
    One by one the moments fall;
Some are coming, some are going;
    Do not strive to grasp them all.
One by one thy duties wait thee —
    Let thy whole strength go to each.
Let no future dreams elate thee,
    Learn thou first what these can teach.

HERVÉ RIEL

On the sea and at the Hogue, sixteen hundred ninety-two,
  Did the English fight the French, — woe to France!
And, the thirty-first of May, helter-skelter through the blue,
Like a crowd of frightened porpoises a shoal of sharks pursue,
  Came crowding ship on ship to St. Malo on the Rance,
With the English fleet in view.
'Twas the squadron that escaped, with the victor in full chase;
  First and foremost of the drove, in his great ship, Damfreville;
    Close on him fled, great and small,
    Twenty-two good ships in all;
And they signaled to the place
" Help the winners of a race!
  Get us guidance, give us harbor, take us quick — or, quicker still,
Here's the English can and will!"
Then the pilots of the place put out brisk and leapt on board;
  "Why, what hope or chance have ships like these to pass?" laughed they: —

"Rocks to starboard, rocks to port, all the passage
    scarred and scored,
Shall the *Formidable* here with her twelve and eighty
    guns
  Think to make the river mouth by the single narrow way,
Trust to enter where 'tis ticklish for a craft of twenty
    tons,
        And with flow at full beside?
        Now, 'tis slackest ebb of tide.
  Reach the mooring? Rather say,
While rock stands or water runs,
Not a ship will leave the bay!"
  Then was called a council straight.
Brief and bitter the debate:
"Here's the English at our heels; would you have
    them take in tow
All that's left us of the fleet, linked together stern
    and bow,
For a prize to Plymouth Sound?
Better run the ships aground!"
  (Ended Damfreville his speech.)
Not a minute more to wait!
  "Let the Captains all and each
  Shove ashore, then blow up, burn the vessels on
    the beach!
France must undergo her fate.

* * * * *

"Give the word!" But no such word
Was ever spoke or heard;
   For up stood, for out stepped, for in struck amid all these
   — A Captain? A Lieutenant? A Mate — first, second, third?
   No such man of mark, and meet
   With his betters to compete!
   But a simple Breton sailor pressed by Tourville for the fleet,
A poor coasting pilot he, Hervé Riel the Croisickese.

And "What mockery or malice have we here?" cries Hervé Riel: —
   "Are you mad, you Malouins? Are you cowards, fools, or rogues?
Talk to me of rocks and shoals, me who took the soundings, tell
On my fingers every bank, every shallow, every swell
   'Twixt the offing here and Grève where the river disembogues?
Are you bought by English gold? Is it love the lying's for?
      Morn and eve, night and day,
      Have I piloted your bay,
Entered free and anchored fast at the foot of Solidor.

"Burn the fleet and ruin France? That were worse
   than fifty Hogues!
  Sirs, they know I speak the truth! Sirs, believe
   me, there's a way!
Only let me lead the line,
  Have the biggest ship to steer,
  Get this *Formidable* clear,
Make the others follow mine,
And I lead them, most and least, by a passage I know
   well,
  Right to Solidor past Grève,
   And there lay them safe and sound;
  And if one ship misbehave,
   — Keel so much as grate the ground,
Why, I've nothing but my life, — here's my head!"
   cries Hervé Riel.
Not a minute more to wait.
"Steer us in, then, small and great!
  Take the helm, lead the line, save the squadron!"
   cried its chief.
"Captains, give the sailor place!
  He is Admiral, in brief."

Still the north wind, by God's grace!
See the noble fellow's face,
As the big ship with a bound
Clears the entry like a hound,

Keeps the passage as its inch of way were the wide
    seas profound !
  See, safe through shoal and rock,
  How they follow in a flock,
Not a ship that misbehaves, not a keel that grates
    the ground,
  Not a spar that comes to grief !
The peril, see, is past,
All are harbored to the last,
And just as Hervé Riel hollas "Anchor!" — sure as
    fate
Up the English come, — too late !
  So, the storm subsides to calm :
They see the green trees wave
On the heights o'erlooking Grève.
  Hearts that bled are stanched with balm.
" Just our rapture to enhance,
  Let the English rake the bay,
Gnash their teeth and glare askance,
  As they cannonade away !
'Neath rampired Solidor pleasant riding on the
    Rance ! "
How hope succeeds despair on each Captain's coun-
    tenance !
Out burst all with one accord,
    "Let France, let France's King
    Thank the man that did the thing ! "

What a shout, and all one word,
    "Hervé Riel!"
As he stepped in front once more,
  Not a symptom of surprise
  In the frank blue Breton eyes,
Just the same man as before.

Then said Damfreville : " My friend,
I must speak out at the end,
  Though I find the speaking hard.
Praise is deeper than the lips :
You have saved the King his ships,
  You must name your own reward.
'Faith, our sun was near eclipse!
Demand whate'er you will,
France remains your debtor still.
Ask to heart's content and have! or my name's not
    Damfreville."

Then a beam of fun outbroke
On the bearded mouth that spoke,
As the honest heart laughed through
Those frank eyes of Breton blue : —
"Since I needs must say my say,
  Since on board the duty's done,
  And from Malo Roads to Croisic Point, what is it
    but a run ? —
Since 'tis ask and have, I may—

  Since the others go ashore —
Come! A good whole holiday!
  Leave to go and see my wife, whom I call the
    Belle Aurore!"
That he asked and that he got, — nothing more,
Name and deed alike are lost:
Not a pillar nor a post
  In his Croisic keeps alive the feat as it befell;
Not a head in white and black
On a single fishing smack,
In memory of the man but for whom had gone to
  wrack
  All that France saved from the fight whence
    England bore the bell.

Go to Paris: rank on rank
  Search the heroes flung pell-mell
On the Louvre, face and flank!
You shall look long enough ere you come to Hervé
  Riel.
So, for better and for worse,
Hervé Riel, accept my verse!
In my verse, Hervé Riel, do thou once more
Save the squadron, honor France, love thy wife, the
  Belle Aurore!
— Robert Browning.

THE STORY OF MY BOYHOOD

My life is a lovely story, happy and full of incident. If, when I was a boy, a good fairy had met me and said, "Choose now thy own course through life, and I will guide and defend thee," my fate could not have been directed more happily.

In the year 1805, there lived in Odense, in a small room, a young married couple. The man was a shoemaker, scarcely twenty-two years old, a man of richly gifted and truly poetical mind. His wife was ignorant of life and of the world, but possessed a heart full of love. The young man had himself made his shoemaking bench, and the furniture with which he began housekeeping.

In this small room, there lay, on the 2d of April, 1805, a living, weeping child, — that was myself, Hans Christian Andersen. During the first day of my existence my father is said to have sat by the bed and read aloud, but I cried all the time.

"Wilt thou go to sleep, or listen quietly?" my father asked in joke; but I still cried on.

Our little room, which was almost filled with the shoemaker's bench and my crib, was the abode of my childhood. The walls were covered with pictures, and over the workbench was a cupboard, containing books and songs. The little kitchen was full of shining plates and metal pans, and by means of a ladder it was possible to go out on the roof. Here there stood a great chest filled with soil, my mother's sole garden, and where she grew her vegetables.

I was the only child, and my father gratified me in all my wishes. I possessed his whole heart. He lived for me. On holidays he made me theaters and pictures, and read to me from the "Arabian Tales."

It was only in such moments as these that I can remember to have seen him really cheerful. His parents had been country people in good circumstances, but upon whom many misfortunes had fallen. The cattle had died; the farmhouse had been burned down; and lastly, his father had lost his reason. On this his mother had removed to Odense, and there put her son, whose mind was full of intelligence, apprentice to a shoemaker. It was my poor father's ardent desire to attend the grammar school where he might learn Latin. But he saw his dearest wish unfulfilled, and he never lost the remembrance of it. I recollect that once, as a child, I saw tears in his eyes, and it was when a youth from the grammar school came to our house and showed us his books and told us what he learned.

On Sundays my father went out into the woods and took me with him. He did not talk much when he was out, but sat silently, sunk in deep thought,

"HOW DARE YOU STRIKE ME?" (See p. 184.)

whilst I ran about and gathered strawberries or bound garlands. Only twice in the year, and that in the month of May, when the woods were arrayed in their earliest green, did my mother go with us. She wore a cotton gown on these occasions, which, as long as I can remember, was her holiday gown. She always took home with her from the wood a great many fresh beech boughs, which were then planted in the garden on the roof.

One of my first recollections had for me a good deal of importance. It was a family festival, and can you guess where? In that very place in Odense which I had always looked on with fear and trembling, — in the Odense House of Correction.

My parents were acquainted with the jailer, who invited them to a family dinner, and I was to go with them. I was at that time still so small that I was carried when I returned home.

The House of Correction was for me a great storehouse of tales about robbers and thieves. Often I had stood, but always at a safe distance, and listened to the singing of the men within and of the women spinning at their wheels.

I went with my parents to the jailer's. The heavy iron-bolted gate was opened and again locked with the key from the rattling bunch. We mounted a steep staircase — we ate and drank, and two of the prisoners waited at the table. They could not induce me to taste of anything. The sweetest things I pushed away. My mother told them I was sick, and I was laid on a bed, where I heard the spinning wheels humming near by and merry singing; but I know that I was afraid all the time. And yet I was in a pleasant humor, making up stories of how I had entered a castle full of robbers. Late in the night my parents went home, carrying me, the rain dashing against my face.

Odense was in my childhood quite another town from what it is now. Then it was a hundred years behind the times. Many customs and manners prevailed which have since disappeared from the capital. When the guilds removed their signs, they went in procession with flying banners and with lemons dressed in ribbons stuck on their swords, led by a harlequin with bells and a wooden sword.

The first Monday in Lent the butchers used to lead through the streets a fat ox, adorned with wreaths of flowers, and ridden by a boy in a white gown and wearing wings.

The sailors also passed through the streets with music and flags and streamers flying. Two of the boldest wrestled on a plank placed between two boats, and the one that did not tumble into the water was the hero.

In my sixth year came the great comet of 1811. My mother told me that it would destroy the earth, or that other horrible things threatened us. I listened to all these stories and fully believed them. With my mother and some of the neighboring women I stood in the churchyard and looked at the frightful and mighty fire ball with its large, shining tail.

All talked about the signs of evil and the day of doom. My father was not of their opinion at all, and gave them a correct and sound explanation. Then my mother sighed, the women shook their heads, and my father laughed and went away. In the evening my mother and my grandmother talked together. I do not know how my grandmother explained it, but I sat in her lap and looked into her mild eyes, and expected every moment that the comet would rush down and the day of judgment come.

The mother of my father came daily to our house, were it only for a moment, in order to see her little grandson, for I was her joy and her delight. Every Sunday evening she brought us some flowers. These adorned my mother's cupboard, but still they were mine; and I was allowed to put them in a glass of water. How great was this pleasure!

I very seldom played with other boys. Even at school I took little interest in their games, but remained sitting within doors. At home I had playthings enough, which my father made for me. I was a singularly dreamy child, and went about with my eyes half-shut.

A teacher, who had an A B C school, taught me the letters, to spell, and to read. She used to have her seat in a high-backed armchair near the clock, from which, at every stroke, some little figures came out. She made use of a big rod, which she always carried with her. The school consisted mostly of girls. It was the custom of the school for all to spell loudly and in as high a key as possible. One day, having got a hit of the rod, I rose immediately, took my book, and went home to my mother. I asked that I might go to another school, and my mother sent me to a school for boys. There was also one girl there, a little one, somewhat older than I. We became very good friends. She used to say that she went to school especially to learn arithmetic, for she could then become dairymaid in some great house.

"That you can become in my castle, when I am a nobleman!" said I, and she laughed at me and told me I was only a poor boy.

I was the smallest in the school, and my teacher always took me by the hand while the other boys played, that I might not be run over. He loved me much, gave me cakes and flowers, and tapped me on the cheeks.

Sometimes, during the harvest, my mother went into the fields to glean. I accompanied her, and we went, like Ruth in the Bible to glean in the rich fields of Boaz. One day we went to a place the bailiff of which was a man of rude and savage disposition. We saw him coming with a huge whip in his hand, and my mother and all the others ran away. I had wooden shoes on my bare feet, and in my haste I lost these, and the thorns pricked me so that I could not run. Thus I was left behind and alone. The man came up and lifted his whip to strike me, when I looked him in the face and exclaimed, —

"How dare you strike me, when God can see it?"

The strong, stern man looked at me, and at once became mild. He patted me on my cheeks, asked me my name, and gave me money.

When I brought the money to my mother and showed it to her, she said to the others, "He is a strange child, my Hans Christian; everybody is kind to him."

My father died while I was still a small boy. When I wept, my mother said, "He is dead, thou needst not call him. The ice maiden has taken him away."

I understood what she meant. I recollected that, in the winter before, when our window panes were frozen, my father had pointed to them and showed us a figure like that of a maiden with outstretched arms.

"She has come to fetch me," said he, in jest. And now, when he lay dead, my mother remembered this, and it was in my thoughts also.

I grew rapidly, and was a tall lad. My mother said that I must not go any longer without an object in life. I was sent, therefore, to the charity school, where I learned religion, writing, and arithmetic.

I had saved a little sum of money, and when I counted it over I found it to be about thirty shillings. I was quite overjoyed at the possession of so much wealth, and I besought my mother that I might make a journey to Copenhagen, to see the greatest city in the world.

"What wilt thou do there?" asked my mother.

"I will be famous," returned I; and then I told her all that I had read about great men. "People have," said I, "at first an immense amount of adversity to go through, and then they will be famous."

At last my mother consented. She packed my clothes in a small bundle, and made a bargain with the driver of a post carriage to take me back with him to Copenhagen. The afternoon on which I was to set out came, and my mother accompanied me to the city gate. Here stood my old grandmother. In the last few years her beautiful hair had become gray. She fell upon my neck and wept, without being able to speak a word. I was myself deeply affected. And thus we parted. I saw her no more, for she died in the following year.

The postilion blew his horn. It was a glorious afternoon, and the sunshine soon entered into my gay, child-like mind.

— HANS CHRISTIAN ANDERSEN.

From " The Story of my Life."

DOUGLAS AND MARMION

THE train from out the castle drew;
But Marmion stopped to bid adieu.
" Though something I might plain," he said,
" Of cold respect to stranger guest,
Sent hither by your king's behest,
While in Tantallon's towers I stayed,
Part we in friendship from your land,
And, noble earl, receive my hand."

But Douglas round him drew his cloak,
Folded his arms, and thus he spoke:
" My manors, halls, and bowers shall still
Be open, at my sovereign's will,
To each one whom he lists, howe'er
Unmeet to be the owner's peer.
My castles are my king's alone,
From turret to foundation stone:
The hand of Douglas is his own,

And never shall, in friendly grasp,
The hand of such as Marmion clasp."

Burned Marmion's swarthy cheek like fire,
And shook his very frame for ire;
　　And "This to me?" he said;
" An 'twere not for thy hoary beard,
Such hand as Marmion's had not spared
　　To cleave the Douglas' head.
And first, I tell thee, haughty peer,
He who does England's message here,
Although the meanest in her state,
May well, proud Angus, be thy mate.

" And, Douglas, more I tell thee here,
　　Even in thy pitch of pride,
Here in thy hold, thy vassals near,
　　I tell thee thou'rt defied!
And if thou saidst I am not peer
To any lord in Scotland here,
Lowland or Highland, far or near,
　　Lord Angus, thou hast lied."

On the earl's cheek the flush of rage
O'ercame the ashen hue of age:
Fierce he broke forth: " And dar'st thou then
To beard the lion in his den,
　　The Douglas in his hall?

And hop'st thou hence unscathed to go?
No, by Saint Bride of Bothwell, no! —
Up drawbridge, grooms! — what, warder, ho!
 Let the portcullis fall."

Lord Marmion turned, — well was his need, —
And dashed the rowels in his steed,
Like arrow through the archway sprung;
The ponderous gate behind him rung:
To pass there was such scanty room,
The bars, descending, grazed his plume.

The steed along the drawbridge flies,
Just as it trembled on the rise;
Nor lighter does the swallow skim
Along the smooth lake's level brim.

And when Lord Marmion reached his band,
He halts, and turns with clenchèd hand,
And shout of loud defiance pours,
And shook his gauntlet at the towers.

— SIR WALTER SCOTT.

From " Marmion."

THE BATTLE OF BLENHEIM

IT was a summer evening,
  Old Kaspar's work was done,
And he, before his cottage door,
  Was sitting in the sun ;
And by him sported on the green,
His little grandchild Wilhelmine.

She saw her brother Peterkin
  Roll something large and round,
Which he beside the rivulet,
  In playing there, had found ;
He came to ask what he had found,
That was so large, and smooth, and round.

Old Kaspar took it from the boy,
  Who stood expectant by ;
And then the old man shook his head,
  And, with a natural sigh,
" 'Tis some poor fellow's skull," said he,
" Who fell in the great victory.

"I find them in the garden,
    For there's many hereabout;
And often when I go to plow,
    The plowshare turns them out;
For many thousand men," said he,
"Were slain in that great victory."

"Now tell us what 'twas all about,"
    Young Peterkin he cries;
While little Wilhelmine looks up
    With wonder-waiting eyes;
"Now tell us all about the war,
And what they killed each other for."

"It was the English," Kaspar cried,
    "Who put the French to rout,
But what they killed each other for,
    I could not well make out;
But everybody said," quoth he,
"That 'twas a famous victory:

"My father lived at Blenheim then,
    Yon little stream, hard by;
They burnt his dwelling to the ground,
    And he was forced to fly;
So, with his wife and child, he fled,
Nor had he where to rest his head.

"With fire and sword, the country round
    Was wasted, far and wide;
And many a nursing mother then,
    And new-born baby, died;
But things like that, you know, must be
At every famous victory.

"They say it was a shocking sight
    After the field was won:
For many thousand bodies here
    Lay rotting in the sun:
But things like that, you know, must be
After a famous victory.

"Great praise the Duke of Marlboro' won,
    And our young prince, Eugene."
"Why, 'twas a very wicked thing!"
    Said little Wilhelmine.
"Nay, nay, my little girl!" quoth he,
"It was a famous victory.

"And everybody praised the Duke
    Who this great fight did win."
"But what good came of it at last?"
    Quoth little Peterkin.
"Why, that I cannot tell," said he,
"But 'twas a glorious victory."

                   — ROBERT SOUTHEY.

BURIAL OF SIR JOHN MOORE

Not a drum was heard, not a funeral note,
    As his corse to the rampart we hurried;
Not a soldier discharged his farewell shot
    O'er the grave where our hero we buried.

We buried him darkly, at dead of night,
    The sods with our bayonets turning,
By the struggling moonbeam's misty light,
    And the lantern dimly burning.

No useless coffin inclosed his breast,
    Nor in sheet nor in shroud we wound him;
But he lay, like a warrior taking his rest,
    With his martial cloak around him.

Few and short were the prayers we said,
    And we spoke not a word of sorrow;
But we steadfastly gazed on the face of the dead,
    And we bitterly thought of the morrow.

We thought as we hollowed his narrow bed,
    And smoothed down his lonely pillow,
That the foe and the stranger would tread o'er his head,
    And we far away on the billow!

Lightly they'll talk of the spirit that's gone,
    And o'er his cold ashes upbraid him;
But little he'll reck, if they let him sleep on,
    In the grave where a Briton has laid him!

But half of our heavy task was done
    When the clock tolled the hour for retiring,
And we heard the distant and random gun
    That the foe was sullenly firing.

Slowly and sadly we laid him down,
    From the field of his fame fresh and gory!
We carved not a line, we raised not a stone,
    But we left him alone in his glory.

                  — CHARLES WOLFE.

AMONG THE ICEBERGS

THE moon rose full and clear upon a sea of mystery. The sun had set behind a black line on our port quarter as we were headed northeast for the passage of Davis Strait to the coast of Greenland. For a moment there was a flush upon the sea, forming a radiance about the icebergs, then across the dark water fell a glittering path of silver, and everywhere were vast, ghostly figures unmoving in the moonlight. The ice was thickening about us. Ahead and upon our starboard quarter it stood in mass, in irregular broken outline, and might have been a great white city upon a plain. Very menacing it looked to us who had gained our dread of ice in trips across the North Atlantic. But there was reassuring unconcernedness on the part of those who had been in these waters before, especially the captain and the crew.

At midnight I was wakened by the clash of collision and a shudder which went through the vessel like the shake of ague. There was a shouting on the deck, and a loud grating of ice along the vessel's side which sounded like sure destruction. Then followed another clash and quiver and more shouting, but the sense of danger was gone, for it was instantly apparent that we were but forcing a way through the floe. It was interesting then to wait for the moment of impact, and the jar which set the vessel trembling in every fiber, and the heave as her bows rose upon an obstructive pan, and the thunder of the pack along her sides, and over all the crescendo of shouting.

Soon it became intelligible. "Starboard!" came faintly from the forward crow's-nest, whence the mate was picking a course through the floe. "Starboard!!" next in a ringing order from the captain on the bridge. "Starboard!!!" finally in a prolonged response from the two men at the wheel at the head of the companionway. Then, "Steady!"

AMONG THE ICEBERGS.

forward from aloft, and "Stead-e-e!!" from the bridge, and a long-drawn "Stead-e-e-e-e!!!" from the men, as the wheel whirled under the release of tension.

From the deck, in the morning, the ship appeared to be imprisoned in a sea of ice; not the black-blue ice of a fresh-water lake, but ice of unspotted white like that of a glacier. In masses of irregular size, known to the sealers as "pans," and of relatively flat surface, it floated about us, broken in uniformity only here and there by the towering bulk of an iceberg. On every side it spread to the horizon, with threadlike branching blue veins of open water among the pans widening now and again to pools that in the sunlight were sapphires set among diamonds.

The *Diana* was having much her own way in a fast-melting summer floe, that drifts from Hudson Bay in the southward Labrador current. Had it been winter, and had she been nipped in the pack and exposed to its terrible lateral pressure, she would have been crushed like an eggshell between the lips of a vise.

In the middle of the morning the sharp eyes of the watch caught sight of open water ahead, and at little after noon we steamed clear of the ice and again set a straight northeasterly course.

One day more of calm and of sunlit seas, then two

of dark, tempestuous weather, with dire discomfort in Davis Strait, and we wakened on Saturday to the welcome sense of an even keel.

Icebergs were many about us. From their cold surfaces the sun was breeding a fog which, even as I watched, shut out the land, and veiled us in a mist through which we could see only a hundred yards across the water. Overhead was clear sky, and in the dense fog to port was a luminous point formed by the sun rays in the mist. This the seamen called a "fog eater." But the promise of clearing which it held was borne out in the course of the morning only by an occasional thinning of the fog, through which we caught furtive glimpses of the mountain tops, with their heights vastly exaggerated, as they appeared above the denser mist that hid the shore.

There is an element of adventure in cruising at full speed in a thick fog along an ill-charted coast, in waters frequented by icebergs as large as St. Peter's Cathedral. We were headed shoreward in the hope of soon running free of fog. From out our easeful attitudes in the sunlight we started suddenly as one man. It was to the call of the captain, who was standing now at the head of the port ladder leading to the bridge, his face livid and his figure bent tensely forward. "Hard a-starboard! Hard a-starboard!" he was shouting in a voice that carried conviction. In an instant the spokes of the double wheel were thick with hands that urged it over at all speed. With the sensitiveness almost of a skiff the *Diana* responded, sweeping, in a great curve, to port, while off our starboard, so near that we could almost toss a biscuit upon it from the deck, rose the ragged peak of a rock projecting a few feet above the water that played about it in dancing ripples.

As suddenly as it closed about us in the early morning the fog lifted in the later afternoon, revealing the coast line through an atmosphere of singular clearness. The sun was late in setting that night. For more than a week we had marked the lengthening days, and it was in keeping with our general good fortune that, in the few hours of darkness each night, the moon should give us ample light until we reached a point where, at that season, the sun would not set at all. It came slowly to its setting now, sloping obliquely well to the north of west, and shedding, far into the night, its level rays across the sea. A faint breeze was blowing from the north, cold from off an ice-cold sea, but surcharged with a quality of vigor that set one's blood bounding. The wind ruffled the placid water as it reflected the red and gold and orange and purple of a sunset which framed the icebergs and the distant snows in a radiance of Italian pink. Fairly in the eye of the setting sun a sportsman in the foretop was first to see a sail, and almost simultaneously he raised a cry of " Whales to starboard!" For half an hour we watched them from the deck. They were three or four " right " whales at play about us, their massive black bulks rising from the gorgeous sea in a movement of great dignity and grace, then disappearing with a flap of the tail that lashed the sea into foam, only to rise again a moment later exhaling hot breath, which in the cold air turned instantly to vapor and shot upward in white spray like the spout of a fountain.

There was no darkness. The mystic twilight of the north fell upon us with the disappearing of the sun. The breeze had died away and the restfulness of perfect calm was upon land and sea, while over all, like an impalpable veil, fell the light that dims the sordid face of things and reveals the mystery and the wonder of the world, and fills us with ineffable regret and longing.

All day we sailed in view of our first Greenland haven. It was a cloudless day, with radiant sea and air, and a grateful warmth that made each quickening breath almost intoxicating. Far to the north, projecting from the mainland, with blue sky above and blue water beneath, we could see from early morning in clear mirage the precipitous cliffs above the harbor of Godhavn. Here were low-lying, lichen-covered rocks, almost level with the sea, and icebergs innumerable. It was an arctic scene far beyond imagining: a sky of warmth and color, a sea of the limpid, placid blue of the tropics, while in it, "ice, mast high, went floating by," not "green as emerald," but white, unmixed, undazzling white, "so as no fuller on earth could white it."

Nearer and nearer we drew to the rock-ribbed, ice-encompassed shore. One always feels a quickening of the pulses in approaching a strange coast, even on the main-traveled highways of the world, but we were nearing now a land which had been visited by relatively few white men since its Norse civilization was destroyed and William Baffin made it known again to the modern world. To our minds it was associated only with all the romance and heroism and adventure of the seekers for the northwest passage and for the pole, by what explorers have called the "American route." A land of unfathomable wonder it seemed to us, where day is an unbroken brightness for half the year and night a darkness for the other half, tempered only by the light of moon and stars; where a dwarfish race dress themselves in the furs of the animals upon which they feed, and lead a life whose conditions are wholly unrealized in the common lot of men.

— WALTER A. WYCKOFF.

From "With Arctic Highlanders," by permission.

PASSING THE ICEBERGS

A FEARLESS shape of brave device,
  Our vessel drives through mist and rain,
Between the floating fleets of ice —
  The navies of the northern main.

These arctic ventures, blindly hurled,
  The proofs of nature's olden force,
Like fragments of a crystal world,
  Long shattered from its skyey course.

These are the buccaneers that fright
  The middle sea with dream of wrecks,
And freeze the south winds in their flight,
  And chain the Gulf Stream to their decks.

At every dragon prow and helm
  There stands some viking as of yore;
Grim heroes from the boreal realm
  Where Odin rules the spectral shore.

And oft beneath the sun or moon
  Their swift and eager falchions glow,
While, like a storm-vexed wind, the rune
  Comes chafing through some beard of snow.

And when the far north flashes up
   With fires of mingled red and gold,
They know that many a blazing cup
   Is brimming to the absent bold.

Up signal then, and let us hail
   Yon looming phantom as we pass!
Note all her fashion, hull, and sail,
   Within the compass of your glass.

See at her mast the steadfast glow
   Of that one star of Odin's throne;
Up with our flag, and let us show
   The constellation on our own.

And speak her well; for she might say,
   If from her heart the words could flow,
Great news from some far frozen bay,
   Or the remotest Eskimo;

Might tell of channels yet untold,
   That sweep the pole from sea to sea;
Of lands which God designs to hold
   A mighty people yet to be;

Of wonders which alone prevail,
   Where day and darkness dimly meet;
Of all which spreads the arctic sail;
   Of Franklin and his venturous fleet;

How, haply, at some glorious goal
   His anchor holds — his sails are furled;
That Fame has named him on her scroll,
   "Columbus of the Polar World."

Or how his plowing barks wedge on
   Through splintering fields with battered shares,
Lit only by that spectral dawn,
   The mask that mocking darkness wears;

Or how, o'er embers black and few,
   The last of shivered masts and spars,
He sits among his frozen crew
   In council with the norland stars.

No answer — but the swollen flow
   Of ocean heaving long and vast; —
An argosy of ice and snow,
   The voiceless north swings proudly past.
                    — T. BUCHANAN READ.

WHY does the sea moan evermore?
Shut out from heaven it makes its moan,
It frets against the boundary shore;
All earth's full rivers cannot fill
The sea, that drinking thirsteth still.
                    — CHRISTINA G. ROSSETTI.

RIP VAN WINKLE

Rip Van Winkle was a good-natured, shiftless man who lived during the old colonial times in a village at the foot of the Catskills. One day, with his dog and gun, he wandered far up the mountains, and there meeting with some strange dwarfs, he fell into a deep sleep which lasted twenty years. When he awoke it seemed to him that only one night had passed. But, in truth, he had become an old man, his beard had grown long, and his clothes had fallen into tatters. He made his way slowly to the village, wondering what had happened.

* * * * *

There was, as usual, a crowd of folk about the door of the inn, but none that Rip recollected. The very character of the people seemed changed. There was a busy, bustling, disputatious tone about it, instead of the accustomed phlegm and drowsy tranquillity. He looked in vain for the sage Nicholas Vedder, with his broad face, double chin, and fair long pipe, uttering clouds of tobacco smoke, instead of idle speeches; or Van Bummel, the schoolmaster, doling forth the contents of an ancient newspaper.

In place of these, a lean, bilious-looking fellow, with his pocket full of handbills, was haranguing vehemently about rights of citizens, elections, members of

THE RETURN OF RIP VAN WINKLE.

Congress, liberty, Bunker's Hill, heroes of seventy-six, and other words, which were a perfect Babylonish jargon to the bewildered Van Winkle.

The appearance of Rip, with his long, grizzled beard, his rusty fowling piece, his uncouth dress, and an army of women and children at his heels, soon attracted the attention of the tavern politicians. They crowded round him, eying him from head to foot with great curiosity. The orator bustled up to him, and, drawing him partly aside, inquired on which side he voted. Rip stared in vacant stupidity. Another short but busy little fellow pulled him by the arm, and, rising on tiptoe, inquired in his ear whether he was Federal or Democrat.

Rip was equally at a loss to comprehend the question, when a knowing, self-important old gentleman, in a sharp cocked hat, made his way through the crowd, putting them to right and left with his elbows as he passed, and, planting himself before Van Winkle, with one arm akimbo, the other resting on his cane, demanded, in an austere tone, what brought him to the election with a gun on his shoulder and a mob at his heels, and whether he meant to breed a riot in the village. "Alas! gentlemen," cried Rip, somewhat dismayed, "I am a poor, quiet man, a native of the place, and a loyal subject of the King, God bless him!"

Here a general shout burst from the bystanders:
"A Tory! a Tory! a spy! a refugee! hustle him!
away with him!" It was with great difficulty that
the self-important man in the cocked hat restored order; and, having assumed a tenfold austerity of brow,
demanded again of the unknown culprit what he
came there for, and whom he was seeking. The poor
man humbly assured him that he meant no harm, but
merely came there in search of some of his neighbors,
who used to keep about the tavern.

"Well, who are they? name them."

Rip bethought himself a moment, and inquired,
"Where's Nicholas Vedder?" There was a silence for
a little while, when an old man replied, in a thin, piping voice, "Nicholas Vedder! why, he is dead and gone
these eighteen years! There was a wooden tombstone in the churchyard that used to tell all about
him, but that's rotten and gone too." "Where's
Brom Dutcher?" "Oh, he went off to the army in
the beginning of the war. Some say he was killed
at the storming of Stony Point; others say he was
drowned in a squall at the foot of Anthony's Nose.
I don't know; he never came back again."

"Where's Van Bummel, the schoolmaster?" "He
went off to the wars, too; was a great militia general,
and is now in Congress." Rip's heart died away at
hearing of these sad changes in his home and friends,

and finding himself thus alone in the world. Every answer puzzled him, too, by treating of such enormous lapses of time, and of matters which he could not understand, — war, Congress, Stony Point. He had no courage to ask after any more friends, but cried out in despair, " Does nobody here know Rip Van Winkle ? "

" Oh, Rip Van Winkle ! " exclaimed two or three. " Oh, to be sure ! That's Rip Van Winkle, yonder, leaning against the tree." Rip looked, and beheld a precise counterpart of himself as he went up the mountain ; apparently as lazy, and certainly as ragged. The poor fellow was now completely confounded; he doubted his own identity, and whether he was himself or another man. In the midst of his bewilderment, the man in the cocked hat demanded who he was, and what was his name.

" God knows ! " exclaimed he, at his wits' end. " I'm not myself, — I'm somebody else. That's me yonder, — no, that's somebody else got into my shoes. I was myself last night, but I fell asleep on the mountain, and they've changed my gun, and everything's changed, and I'm changed, and I can't tell what's my name, or who I am ! "

The bystanders began now to look at each other, nod, wink significantly, and tap their fingers against their foreheads. There was a whisper, also, about securing the gun, and keeping the old fellow from doing mischief, at the very suggestion of which the self-important man in the cocked hat retired with some precipitation. At this critical moment a fresh, comely woman pressed through the throng to get a peep at the gray-bearded man. She had a chubby child in her arms, which, frightened at his looks, began to cry. "Hush, Rip!" cried she; "hush! the old man won't hurt you."

The name of the child, the air of the mother, the tone of her voice, all awakened a train of recollections in his mind. "What is your name, my good woman?" asked he. "Judith Gardenier." "And your father's name?" "Ah, poor man! Rip Van Winkle was his name, but it's twenty years since he went away from home with his gun, and has never been heard of since. His dog came home without him; but whether he shot himself, or was carried away by the Indians, nobody can tell. I was then but a little girl."

Rip had but one question more to ask, but he put it with a faltering voice: "Where's your mother?" "Oh, she too had died but a short time since; she broke a blood vessel in a fit of passion at a New England peddler." There was a drop of comfort, at least, in this intelligence. The honest man could contain himself no longer. He caught his daughter and her child in his arms. "I am your father!" cried he.

"Young Rip Van Winkle once, old Rip Van Winkle now! Does nobody know poor Rip Van Winkle?"

All stood amazed, until an old woman, tottering out from among the crowd, put her hand to her brow and, peering under it in his face for a moment, exclaimed, "Sure enough! it is Rip Van Winkle! it is himself. Why, where have you been these twenty long years?" Rip's story was soon told, for the whole twenty years had been to him but as one night.

To make a long story short, the company broke up, and returned to the more important concerns of the election. Rip's daughter took him home to live with her. She had a snug, well-furnished house, and a stout, cheery farmer for a husband. Rip soon found many of his former cronies; but preferred making friends among the rising generation, with whom he soon grew into great favor.

Adapted from "The Sketch Book." — WASHINGTON IRVING.

THE BELLS

HEAR the sledges with the the bells,
    Silver bells!
What a world of merriment their melody foretells!
  How they tinkle, tinkle, tinkle,
    In the icy air of night!
  While the stars, that oversprinkle
  All the heavens, seem to twinkle

With a crystalline delight;
Keeping time, time, time,
In a sort of Runic rhyme,
To the tintinnabulation that so musically wells
From the bells, bells, bells, bells,
Bells, bells, bells —
From the jingling and the tinkling of the bells.

Hear the mellow wedding bells,
Golden bells!
What a world of happiness their harmony foretells!
Through the balmy air of night
How they ring out their delight!
From the molten-golden notes,
And all in tune,
What a liquid ditty floats
To the turtle-dove that listens, while she gloats
On the moon!

Oh, from out the sounding cells,
What a gush of euphony voluminously wells!
How it swells!
How it dwells
On the future! how it tells
Of the rapture that impels
To the swinging and the ringing
Of the bells, bells, bells,

Of the bells, bells, bells, bells,
        Bells, bells, bells —
To the rhyming and the chiming of the bells!

Hear the loud alarum bells,
        Brazen bells!
What a tale of terror, now, their turbulency tells!
    In the startled ear of night
    How they scream out their affright!
      Too much horrified to speak,
      They can only shriek, shriek,
        Out of tune,
In a clamorous appealing to the mercy of the fire,
In a mad expostulation with the deaf and frantic fire,
      Leaping higher, higher, higher,
      With a desperate desire,
    And a resolute endeavor
    Now — now to sit or never,
    By the side of the pale-faced moon.

    Oh, the bells, bells, bells!
    What a tale their terror tells
        Of Despair!
    How they clang, and clash, and roar!
    What a horror they outpour
On the bosom of the palpitating air!
    Yet the ear it fully knows,

>   By the twanging
>   And the clanging,
>   How the danger ebbs and flows;
>   Yet the ear distinctly tells,
>   In the jangling,
>   And the wrangling,
>   How the danger sinks and swells,
> By the sinking or the swelling in the anger of the bells,
>   Of the bells,
>   Of the bells, bells, bells, bells,
>   Bells, bells bells —
> In the clamor and the clangor of the bells.
>
> —Edgar Allan Poe.

LITTLE GAVROCHE

Years ago there might have been noticed on the streets of Paris a boy of eleven or twelve years of age, who was known by the name of Little Gavroche. This child was dressed in a man's trousers and a woman's jacket, in which some kind persons had clothed him out of charity.

Little Gavroche was never so comfortable anywhere as in the street. He was a noisy, pale, active, sharp, impudent lad, with a cunning and sickly look. He came and went, sang, played at hopscotch, searched the gutters, stole a little, but gayly, like cats and sparrows, laughed when he was called a scamp, and felt angry when he was called a thief. He had no bed, no bread, no fire, no love; but he was happy because he was free.

One evening in the early spring, when the breezes were blowing sharply, so sharply that January seemed to have returned, and the citizens had put on their cloaks again, little Gavroche, still shivering gayly under his rags, was standing as if in ecstasy in front of a hairdresser's shop. He was adorned with a woolen shawl, picked up no one knew where, of which he had made a muffler. Little Gavroche appeared to be lost in admiration of a waxen image of a bride, with a wreath of orange blossoms in her hair, which revolved between two lamps in the window. But in reality he was watching the shop to see whether he could not snatch a cake of soap, which he would afterward sell to a barber in the suburbs.

While Gavroche was examining the bride, the window, and the soap, he saw two boys, very decently dressed, both younger than himself, timidly open the door and enter the shop. They both spoke together, asking for charity. Their words were unintelligible, because sobs choked the voice of the younger boy and cold made the teeth of the elder rattle. The barber, without laying down his razor, drove them into the street, and closed the door.

The two lads set off again, crying. A cloud had come up in the meanwhile, and rain began to fall. Little Gavroche ran up to them.

"What is the matter with you?" he asked.

"We don't know where to sleep," the elder replied.

"Is that all?" said Gavroche. "Is that anything to cry about, simpletons?" And assuming an accent of tender care and gentle protection, he said, —

"Come with me, boys."

"Yes, sir," said the elder boy.

And the two children followed him as they would have done an archbishop, and left off crying.

As they went along the street, Gavroche noticed a little girl shivering in a gateway.

"Poor girl," said Gavroche. "Here, take this."

And taking off the good woolen garment which he had around his neck he threw it over the thin, bare shoulders of the beggar girl, where the muffler became once again a shawl. The little girl looked at him with an astonished air, and received the shawl in silence.

The shower, redoubling its passion, poured down.

"Hello!" Gavroche shouted. "What's the meaning of this? It is raining again."

And he went on, shivering with the cold.

"No matter," he said, as he took a glance at the beggar girl crouching under her shawl, "she's got something to cover her anyway."

The two children limped after him, and as they passed a baker's shop, Gavroche turned round.

"By the by, boys, have you dined?"

"We have had nothing to eat, sir, since early this morning," the elder answered.

Gavroche stopped, and for some minutes searched through his rags. At length he raised his head with an air of triumph, —

"Calm yourselves; here is supper for three;" and he drew a coin from one of his pockets. Without giving the lads time to feel amazed, he pushed them both before him into the baker's shop, and laid his money on the counter, exclaiming, —

"Bread for three!"

When the bread was cut, Gavroche said to the two boys, —

"Eat away."

At the same time he gave each of them a lump of bread. There was one piece smaller than the two others, and he took that for himself. Then he said, —

"Let us return to the street," and they started again in the direction of the Bastile. From time to time, as they passed lighted shops, the younger boy stopped to see what time it was.

* * * * * * *

Some years back there might have been seen in the southeastern corner of the square of the Bastile a quaint monument. It was an elephant, forty feet high, constructed of carpentry and masonry. On its back it bore a castle which resembled a house, once painted green by some plasterer, and now painted black by the rain and by time.

In this deserted corner of the square, the wide forehead of the elephant, its trunk, its tusks, its castle, its enormous back, and its four feet, like columns, produced at night a surprising and terrible outline. No one knew what it meant, and no passer-by looked at it. It was falling in ruins, and each season, plaster becoming detached from its flanks, made horrible wounds upon it. It was to this huge structure that Gavroche led the two urchins.

On coming near the colossus, Gavroche understood the effect which the very great may produce on the very little, and said, —

"Don't be frightened, little ones."

A ladder, used by workmen during the day, was lying near the monument. Gavroche raised it with singular vigor and placed it against one of the elephant's fore legs. At the point where the ladder ended, a sort of black hole could be distinguished in the body of the colossus. Gavroche pointed out the ladder and the hole to his guests, and said, —

"Go up, and go in." The two little boys looked at each other in terror.

"You are frightened!" Gavroche exclaimed, and added, "You shall see."

He clung around the elephant's wrinkled foot, and in a twinkling, without deigning to use the ladder, he reached the hole. He went in like a lizard gliding into a crevice, and a moment after the boys saw his head appear on the edge of the hole.

"Well," he cried, "come up, my blessed babes. You will see how snug it is. Come up, you," he said to the elder. "I will hold your hand."

The elder boy ventured, and the younger, on seeing himself left alone between the feet of this great beast, felt much inclined to cry, but did not dare. The elder climbed up the rungs of the ladder in a very tottering way, and as he did so Gavroche encouraged him by exclaiming, —

"Don't be frightened! That is it — keep on moving; set your foot there; now your hand here — bravo!"

And when he was within reach, Gavroche quickly and powerfully seized him by the arm and drew him in.

"Swallowed!" he said. The boy had passed through the crevice.

"Now," said Gavroche, "wait for me. Pray sit down, sir."

And leaving the hole in the same way as he had

entered it, he slid down the elephant's leg with the agility of a monkey, and fell on his feet in the grass. Seizing the younger boy around the waist, he planted him in the middle of the ladder. Then he began ascending behind him, shouting to the elder boy, —

"I'll push him and you pull him."

In a second the little fellow was pushed, dragged, pulled, and drawn through the hole, before he knew where he was; and Gavroche, entering after him, kicked away the ladder, and clapped his hands as he shouted, —

"There we are! Long live General Lafayette!" This explosion over, he added, —

"Boys, you are in my house."

Gavroche was, in fact, at home. Oh, goodness of the giants! This huge monument had become the lodging of a waif. The people who passed by the elephant of the Bastile were prone to look at it scornfully and say, —

"Of what use is that?"

Yet it served to save from cold, from frost, from damp, from wind and rain, a little fatherless, motherless boy, without bread, clothes, or shelter.

The hole by which Gavroche entered was scarcely visible from the outside, as it was concealed under the elephant's body, and so narrow that only cats and boys could pass through it.

"Let us begin," said Gavroche, "by telling the porter that we are not at home."

And plunging into the darkness, he took a plank and stopped up the hole. Gavroche plunged again into the darkness. The children heard the fizzing of a match. A sudden light made them wink. Gavroche had lit a bit of string dipped in pitch, and this thing, which gave more smoke than light, made the inside of the elephant indistinctly visible.

An entire gigantic skeleton was to be seen. The pieces which had fallen from the elephant's back had filled up the cavity, so that it was possible to walk on it as on a flooring.

Gavroche's two guests looked fearfully into the dark corners. The younger lad nudged his brother and said, —

"How black it is!"

This remark made Gavroche cry out, —

"It is outside that it is black. Outside it rains, and here it does not rain. Outside it is cold, and here there is not a breath of wind. Outside there is not even the moon, and here there is a candle."

The two lads began looking around the apartment with less terror, but Gavroche did not allow them any time for meditation.

"Quick!" he said. And he thrust them toward that end of the room where his bed was.

Gavroche's bed had a mattress, a coverlet, and an alcove with curtains. The mattress was a straw mat, and the coverlet was a blanket of coarse gray wool, very warm, and nearly new. This is what the alcove was, — three long props were driven into the plaster soil, two in front and one behind, so as to form a hollow pyramid. These props supported a grating of brass wire that entirely surrounded the three poles. A row of large stones fastened the latticework down to the ground, so that nothing could pass.

Gavroche's bed was under the wirework, as in a cage, and the whole resembled an Eskimo's tent. Gavroche moved a few of the stones that held down the latticework in front, and shouted to the lads, —

"Now then, crawl in."

He made his guests enter the cage cautiously, then went in after them, brought the stones together again, and closed the opening. They lay down all three on the mat. Gavroche still held the candle in his hand.

"Now," he said, "go to sleep; I am going to put out the light."

"What is that for, sir?" the elder of the lads asked Gavroche, pointing to the brass grating.

"That," said Gavroche, gravely, "is on account of the rats. Go to sleep!"

Still he continued, —

"It came from the park, and is employed to guard ferocious animals."

While speaking, Gavroche wrapped up the little boy in the blanket, who murmured, —

"Oh, that is nice, it is so warm!"

Gavroche took a glance of satisfaction at the coverlet.

"That also comes from the park," he said; "I took it from the monkeys."

And pointing out to the elder one the thick straw mat on which he was lying, he added, —

"That belonged to the giraffe."

After a pause he continued, —

"The beasts had all these things, and I took them from them. They were not at all angry, for I told them that I wanted them for the elephant."

The younger lad had his eyes wide open, but said nothing. As he was on the edge of the mat, the elder being in the center, Gavroche tucked the coverlet around him as a mother would have done. Then he turned to the elder boy.

"Well, it is jolly here, is it not?"

"Oh, yes," the lad answered, as he looked at Gavroche gratefully.

The two poor little fellows, who had been wet through, began to grow warm again. At this moment a drop of pitch fell on Gavroche's hand.

"See!" he said, "the match is wearing out. Pay attention! When people go to bed they are expected to go to sleep."

The storm grew more furious, and through the thunder peals the rain could be heard pattering on the back of the colossus.

"Wrap yourselves well in the blanket, children," said Gavroche, "for I am going to put the light out. Are you all right?"

"Yes," said the elder boy, "I am all right, and feel as if I had a feather pillow under my head."

The two lads crept close together; Gavroche made them comfortable on the mat, and pulled the blanket up to their ears. Then he repeated for the third time, —

"Go to sleep."

And he blew out the rope's end. The light was scarce extinguished before a singular trembling began to shake the trelliswork under which the three children were lying. It was a multitude of dull rubbings, as if claws and teeth were assailing the copper wire. This was accompanied by all sorts of little shrill cries.

The little boy of five years of age, hearing this noise above his head, was chilled with terror. He nudged his elder brother, but he was sleeping already, as Gavroche had ordered him. Then the little one, unable to hold out any longer for fright, dared to address Gavroche, but in a very low voice.

"Sir?"

"Hello!" said Gavroche, who had just closed his eyes.

"What is that?"

"It's the rats," Gavroche answered. And he laid his head again on the mat.

"Sir?" he began again.

"Well?" Gavroche asked.

"What are rats?"

"They are mice."

This explanation slightly reassured the child, for he had seen white mice in his life and had not been afraid of them. Still, he trembled with fear.

"Don't be frightened," said Gavroche, "they can't get in. And then, I am here. Stay; take my hand; hold your tongue and go to sleep."

The night hours passed away; darkness covered the immense Bastile square. A winter wind, which was mingled with rain, blew in gusts. The patrols examined doors and dark corners, searching for vagabonds, and passed silently before the elephant. The monster, erect and motionless, with its eyes open in the darkness, sheltered from the sky and rain the three poor sleeping children. — VICTOR HUGO.

From " Les Misérables."

ORATION OF MARK ANTONY

Friends, Romans, countrymen, lend me your ears;
I come to bury Cæsar, not to praise him.
The evil that men do, lives after them;
The good is oft interred with their bones;
So let it be with Cæsar! The noble Brutus
Hath told you, Cæsar was ambitious:
If it were so, it were a grievous fault,
And grievously hath Cæsar answered it.
Here, under leave of Brutus and the rest,
(For Brutus is an honorable man;
So are they all, all honorable men;)
Come I to speak in Cæsar's funeral.
He was my friend, faithful and just to me:
But Brutus says he was ambitious;
And Brutus is an honorable man.
He hath brought many captives home to Rome,
Whose ransoms did the general coffers fill:
Did this in Cæsar seem ambitious?
When that the poor have cried, Cæsar hath wept;
Ambition should be made of sterner stuff;
Yet Brutus says he was ambitious;
And Brutus is an honorable man.
You all did see, that, on the Lupercal,
I thrice presented him a kingly crown,
Which he did thrice refuse. Was this ambition?

Yet Brutus says he was ambitious,
And sure, he is an honorable man.
I speak not to disprove what Brutus spake,
But here I am to speak what I do know.
You all did love him once, not without cause;
What cause withholds you, then, to mourn for him?
O judgment, thou art fled to brutish beasts,
And men have lost their reason! Bear with me;
My heart is in the coffin, there, with Cæsar,
And I must pause till it come back to me.

*　　　*　　　*　　　*　　　*　　　*　　　*

But yesterday, the word of Cæsar might
Have stood against the world; now lies he there,
And none so poor to do him reverence.
O masters! if I were disposed to stir
Your hearts and minds to mutiny and rage,
I should do Brutus wrong, and Cassius wrong,
Who, you all know, are honorable men:
I will not do them wrong; I rather choose
To wrong the dead, to wrong myself and you,
Than I will wrong such honorable men.

But here's a parchment, with the seal of Cæsar;
I found it in his closet, 'tis his will;
Let but the commons hear this testament,
(Which, pardon me, I do not mean to read,)
And they would go and kiss dead Cæsar's wounds
And dip their napkins in his sacred blood;

And, as he plucked his cursed steel away,
Mark how the blood of Cæsar followed it.
This was the most unkindest cut of all;
For, when the noble Cæsar saw him stab,
Ingratitude, more strong than traitors' arms,
Quite vanquished him, then burst his mighty heart;
And, in his mantle muffling up his face,
    Great Cæsar fell.
Oh, what a fall was there, my countrymen!
Then I, and you, and all of us fell down,
Whilst bloody treason flourished over us.
Oh, now you weep; and I perceive you feel
The dint of pity. These are gracious drops.
Kind souls! What, weep you, when you but behold
Our Cæsar's vesture wounded? Look you here.
Here is himself, marred, as you see, by traitors.

 1st Citizen. O piteous spectacle!

 2d Citizen. O noble Cæsar!

 3d Citizen. We will be revenged! Revenge! about,—
Seek, — burn, — fire, — kill, — slay! — let not a traitor live.

 Antony. Good friends, sweet friends, let me not stir you up
To such a sudden flood of mutiny.
They that have done this deed are honorable,
And will, no doubt, with reason answer you.
I came not, friends, to steal away your hearts;

I am no orator, as Brutus is;
But, as you know me all, a plain, blunt man,
That loves my friend; and that they know full well
That gave me public leave to speak of him.
For I have neither wit, nor words, nor worth,
Action, nor utterance, nor the power of speech,
To stir men's blood. I only speak right on:
I tell you that which you yourselves do know;
Show you sweet Cæsar's wounds, poor, poor, dumb
    mouths,
And bid them speak for me. And were I Brutus,
And Brutus Antony, there were an Antony
Would ruffle up your spirits, and put a tongue
In every wound of Cæsar, that should move
The stones of Rome to rise and mutiny.

— SHAKESPEARE.

From " Julius Cæsar."

A DAY IN JUNE

AND what is so rare as a day in June?
    Then, if ever, come perfect days;
Then heaven tries earth if it be in tune,
    And over it softly her warm ear lays:
Whether we look, or whether we listen,
We hear life murmur, or see it glisten;
Every clod feels a stir of might,
    An instinct within it that reaches and towers,

And groping blindly above it for light,
    Climbs to a soul in grass and flowers;
The flush of life may well be seen
    Thrilling back over hills and valleys;
The cowslip startles in meadows green,
    The buttercup catches the sun in its chalice,
And there's never a leaf nor a blade too mean
    To be some happy creature's palace;
The little bird sits at his door in the sun,
    Atilt like a blossom among the leaves,
And lets his illumined being o'errun
    With the deluge of summer it receives;
His mate feels the eggs beneath her wings,
And the heart in her dumb breast flutters and sings;
He sings to the wide world and she to her nest —
In the nice ear of Nature which song is the best?
Now is the high-tide of the year,
    And whatever of life hath ebbed away
Comes flooding back with a rippling cheer,
    Into every bare inlet and creek and bay;
Now the heart is so full that a drop overfills it,
We are happy now because God wills it;
No matter how barren the past may have been,
'Tis enough for us now that the leaves are green;
We sit in the warm shade and feel right well
How the sap creeps up and the blossoms swell;
We may shut our eyes, but we cannot help knowing

That skies are clear and grass is growing;
The breeze comes whispering in our ear,
That dandelions are blossoming near,
    That maize has sprouted, that streams are flowing,
That the river is bluer than the sky,
That the robin is plastering his house hard by;
And if the breeze kept the good news back,
For other couriers we should not lack;
    We could guess it all by yon heifer's lowing —
And hark! how clear bold chanticleer,
Warmed with the new wine of the year,
    Tells all in his lusty crowing!

Joy comes, grief goes, we know not how;
Everything is happy now,
    Everything is upward striving;
'Tis as easy now for the heart to be true
As for the grass to be green or skies to be blue —
    'Tis the natural way of living;
Who knows whither the clouds have fled?
    In the unscarred heaven they leave no wake;
And the eyes forget the tears they have shed,
    The heart forgets its sorrow and ache;
The soul partakes the season's youth,
    And the sulphurous rifts of passion and woe
Lie deep 'neath a silence pure and smooth,
    Like burned-out craters healed with snow.
                      — JAMES RUSSELL LOWELL.

SPEECH AND SILENCE

1. HE who speaks honestly cares not, needs not care, though his words be preserved to remotest time. The dishonest speaker, not he only who purposely utters falsehoods, but he who does not purposely, and with sincere heart, utter Truth, and Truth alone; who babbles he knows not what, and has clapped no bridle on his tongue, but lets it run racket, ejecting chatter and futility, — is among the most indisputable malefactors omitted, or inserted, in the Criminal Calendar.

2. To him that will well consider it, idle speaking is precisely the beginning of all Hollowness, Halfness, Infidelity (want of Faithfulness); the genial atmosphere in which rank weeds of every kind attain the mastery over noble fruits in man's life, and utterly choke them out: one of the most crying maladies of these days, and to be testified against, and in all ways to the uttermost withstood.

3. Wise, of a wisdom far beyond our shallow depth, was that old precept: "Watch thy tongue; out of it are the issues of Life!" Man is properly an *incarnated word:* the *word* that he speaks is the *man* himself. Were eyes put into our head, that we might see, or that we might fancy, and plausibly pretend, we had seen? Was the tongue suspended there, that

it might tell truly what we had seen, and make man the soul's-brother of man; or only that it might utter vain sounds, jargon, soul-confusing, and so divide man, as by enchanted walls of Darkness, from union with man?

4. Thou who wearest that cunning, heaven-made organ, a Tongue, think well of this. Speak not, I passionately entreat thee, till thy thought have silently matured itself, till thou have other than mad and mad-making noises to emit: hold thy tongue till *some* meaning lie behind, to set it wagging.

5. Consider the significance of SILENCE: it is boundless, never by meditating to be exhausted, unspeakably profitable to thee! Cease that chaotic hubbub, wherein thy own soul runs to waste, to confused suicidal dislocation and stupor; out of Silence comes thy strength. "Speech is silvern, Silence is golden; Speech is human, Silence is divine."

6. Fool! thinkest thou that because no one stands near with parchment and blacklead to note thy jargon, it therefore dies and is harmless? Nothing dies, nothing can die. No idlest word thou speakest but is a seed cast into Time, and grows through all Eternity! The Recording Angel, consider it well, is no fable, but the truest of truths.

— THOMAS CARLYLE.

OPPORTUNITY

This I beheld, or dreamed it in a dream:
There spread a cloud of dust along a plain,
And underneath the cloud, or in it, raged
A furious battle, and men yelled, and swords
Shocked upon swords and shields. A prince's banner
Wavered, then staggered backward, hemmed by foes.
A craven hung along the battle's edge,
And thought: "Had I a sword of keener steel —
That blue blade that the king's son bears — but this
Blunt thing ——" he snapped and flung it from his hand,
And, lowering, crept away and left the field.
Then came the king's son, wounded, sore bestead,
And weaponless, and saw the broken sword,
Hilt-buried in the dry and trodden sand,
And ran and snatched it, and with battle shout
Lifted afresh, he hewed his enemy down
And saved a great cause that heroic day.
— EDWARD ROWLAND SILL.

There is a tide in the affairs of men,
Which, taken at the flood, leads on to fortune;
Omitted, all the voyage of their life
Is bound in shallows and in miseries.
— SHAKESPEARE.

THE MYSTERY OF LIFE

Though I am no poet, I have dreams sometimes: — I dreamed I was at a child's May-day party, in which every means of entertainment had been provided for the children by a wise and kind host. It was in a stately house, with beautiful gardens attached to it; and the children had been set free in the rooms and gardens, with no care whatever but how to pass their afternoon rejoicingly.

They did not, indeed, know much about what was to happen next day; and some of them, I thought, were a little frightened, because there was a chance of their being sent to a new school where there were examinations; but they kept the thoughts of that out of their heads as well as they could, and resolved to enjoy themselves. The house, I said, was in a beautiful garden, and in the garden were all kinds of flowers; sweet, grassy banks for rest; and smooth lawns for play; and pleasant streams and woods; and rocky places for climbing.

And the children were happy for a little while, but presently they separated themselves into parties; and then each party declared it would have a piece of the garden for its own, and that none of the others should have anything to do with that piece. Next, they quarreled violently, which pieces they would have; and at last the boys took up the thing, as boys should do, "practically," and fought in the flower beds till there was hardly a flower left standing; then they trampled down each other's bits of the garden out of spite; and the girls cried till they could cry no more; and so they all lay down at last breathless in the ruin, and waited for the time when they were to be taken home in the evening.

Meanwhile, the children in the house had been making themselves happy also in their manner. For them, there had been provided every kind of indoors pleasure: there was music for them to dance to; and the library was open, with all manner of amusing books; and there was a workshop, with lathes and carpenter's tools for the ingenious boys; and there were pretty fantastic dresses, for the girls to dress in; and a table, in the dining room, loaded with everything nice to eat.

But in the midst of all this, it struck two or three of the more practical children, that they would like some of the brass-headed nails that studded the chairs; and so they set to work to pull them out. Presently, the others, who were reading, or looking at shells, took a fancy to do the like; and, in a little while, all the children, nearly, were spraining their fingers in pulling out brass-headed nails. With all that they could pull out, they were not satisfied; and then, everybody wanted some of somebody else's. The really practical and sensible ones declared, that nothing was of any real consequence, that afternoon, except to get plenty of brass-headed nails; and that the books, and the cakes, and the microscopes were of no use at all in themselves, but only if they could be exchanged for nail-heads.

And at last they began to fight for nail-heads, as the others fought for the bits of garden. Only here and there, a despised one shrank away into a corner, and tried to get a little quiet with a book, in the midst of the noise; but all the practical ones thought of nothing else but counting nail-heads all the afternoon — even though they knew they would not be allowed to carry so much as one brass knob away with them.

But no — it was "Who has most nails? I have a hundred, and you have fifty;" or, "I have a thousand and you have two. I must have as many as you before I leave the house, or I cannot possibly go home in peace." At last they made so much noise that I awoke, and thought to myself, "What a false dream that is, of *children*. The child is the father of the man; and wiser. Children never do such foolish things. Only men do."

— JOHN RUSKIN.

OVER THE HILL

"Traveler, what lies over the hill?
   Traveler, tell to me:
I am only a child — from the window sill
   Over I cannot see."

"Child, there's a valley over there,
   Pretty and wooded and shy;
And a little brook that says, 'Take care,
   Or I'll drown you by and by.'"

"And what comes next?" "A little town,
   And a towering hill again;
More hills and valleys, up and down,
   And a river now and then."

"And what comes next?" "A lonely moor
   Without a beaten way;
And gray clouds sailing slow before
   A wind that will not stay."

"And then?" "Dark rocks and yellow sand,
   And a moaning sea beside."
"And then?" "More sea, more sea, more land,
   And rivers deep and wide."

"And then?" "Oh, rock and mountain and vale,
  Rivers and fields and men,
Over and over — a weary tale —
  And round to your home again."
— GEORGE MACDONALD.

THE SUN IS DOWN

The sun is down, and time gone by,
The stars are twinkling in the sky,
The hours have passed with stealthy flight,
We needs must part: Good night, good night!
We part in hopes of days as bright
As this gone by: Good night, good night!
— JOANNA BAILLIE.

FINALE

The play is done — the curtain drops,
  Slowly falling to the prompter's bell;
A moment yet the actor stops,
  And looks around to say farewell.
On life's wide scene you, too, have parts,
  That fate ere long shall bid you play; —
Good night! With honest, gentle hearts
  And kindly greeting, go alway!
— W. M. THACKERAY.

APPENDIX

PRONOUNCING KEY AND WORD LIST

The following key to the pronunciation of words is in accordance with Webster's International Dictionary. The silent letters are printed in italics. As a rule, only accented and doubtful syllables are diacritically marked.

The list includes the proper names, together with such other words as are most likely to be misspelled or mispronounced.

ā	māte	ī	pīne	u̱	ru̱de	ow	cow
ă	măt	ĭ	pĭn	û	fûr	c	can
ä	jär	ī	sīr	u̯	fu̯ll	ç	çent
a̱	ca̱ll			ȳ	mȳ	g	get
â	âir	ō	nōte	y̆	city̆	ġ	ġem
ȧ	ȧsk	ŏ	nŏt	o͞o	mo͞on	s	so
		o̱	do̱	o͝o	fo͝ot	s̱	as̱
ē	wē			oi	oil	ch	chair
ĕ	wĕt	ū	ūse	oy	toy	th	thin
ẽ	hẽr	ŭ	ŭs	ou	out	th̲	th̲em

a̱ = ŏ	what	ȯ = ŭ	sȯn	-tion	=	-shŭn
ã = ẽ	cellãr	ŏ = ẽ	com'fŏrt	-sion	=	-shŭn
ê = â	thêre	ô = a̱	ôr	-s̱ion	=	-zhŭn
e = ā	they	o̱ = o͞o	wo̱lf	-tient	=	-shent
o̱ = o͞o	mo̱ve	ṉ = ng	iṉk	-tious	=	-shŭs

A'bra ham	ăv'a lançhe	Çæ'şar	czär
A bruz'zo	ăz'ure	cam pāign'	
(-brōōtz-)		cañon (căn'yon)	Dạm fre vĭlle'
ac cŏm'pa ni-	bạl'dric	ca păç'i ty	De Kălb'
ment	Bạl'ti more	Căs'si us	dĕl'e gate
a chiēve'	bap tĭş'mal	Ca thāy'	dĕl'i cate ly
A ehĭl'lēş	Bȧs tīle'	Căts'kill	deş hä bĭlle'
Ad'ams	be hāv'ior	cav a liēr'	Dĕv'on shire
à droit'ness	Bĕlle Au rōre'	Çĕ'çil	dis sĕv'er
à lăc'ri ty	bĕl lĭg'er ent	çe lĕr'i ty	dĭ vẽr'sion
A lăs'ka	bĕl'lum	çe lĕs'tial	dŏl'phin
ăn'ces tor	be nĕv'o lent	çĕr'e mo ny	Doŭg'las
An̤'gus	Bẽrke'leў	ehȧ ŏt'ic	dra măt'ic
ap pel lā'tion	bĕv'er age	çhâ teau	du ĕl'lum
ap pre hĕn'-	Blĕn'heīm	(shȧ tō')	
sion	Blount	Çhȧ vän ĭac'	East In'dĭeş
ȧreh'ĭ tecture	Bō'az	Ches'a pēake	ĕl'e ġy
As'a hĕl	Bŏn'ni cas tle	çhĭv'al ry	E lĭz'a beth
as si dū'i ty	Bŏth'well	chŏc'o late	ĕl'o quençe
A thē'nĭ an	Brăn'dy wine	cicala (chĕ kä'lȧ)	em băr'rass
Ath'ens	Bre genz'	co lŏs'sus	en thū'sĭ asm
At'kin son	(-gĕnts)	com pĕt'i tor	Es'kĭ mo
Ä'trĭ	Bret'on (brĭt-)	Cŏn̤'cord	eū'pho ny
at tend'ant	brĭek'kĭln	Cŏn'stançe	ex ĕc'u trĭx
at'ti tude	Brĭt'on	Co pen hā'gen	ex haus'tion
Au'burn	Brŏm Dŭtch'er	Côrn wạl'lis	
Aus trā'li an	Brṳ'tus	coun'ter feit	Fâir'wĕath er
Aus'tri an	brȳ'on y	cou'rĭ er	fạl'con
Au vergne	buoy'ant	Croi sick ēşe'	Făn'euil
(ō vȧrñ')	Bûr goyne'	crȳs'tal line	fĕm'i nine

fĭs′sūre	Ish′ma el īte	Mĭn′den	Plўm′oŭth
frŏl′icked		mĭr′a cle	pôr′poise
fûrze	jŏc′und	mo mĕn′tum	prĕç′ĭ pĭçe
	jū′bi lant	mo nŏt′o nous	prē ma tūre′
Gär′den ier	Jū′däh	Mō′ṣeṣ	pre sāge′
Gȧ rōōp′nȧ	Jū′dith	Mun rōe′	prĭv′ĭ lėġe
Gȧ vrōçhe′		mўr′i ad	pro vĭn′çial
glā′çier	Lăb′ra dor	Mўr′mi dons	
Gloucester	Lä fȧ̊y ĕtte′		Rạ′leigh
(glŏs′ter)	Lē′vi	Nẽr′vĭ ī	Rançe
Gōd′hävn	Lĕx′ing ton	Nieh′o las	Răv′e loe
Green′land	liēġe′man		rĕc′on çile
Grève (grĕv)	Lis soy′	O′dĕn se	Re Giȯ vȧn′nĭ
	Loụ′is bûrg	O′din	Reụ′ben
Hăd′leў	Loụ′vre	oụ′zel	re vẽr′ber ate
hăg′gard	Lū′per cạl		rĕv′er end
Hăn′cock		păr′a ble	rĭd′ĭ cūle
Hăr′ring ton	Mä′lo	păr′al lel	Riēl
Hẽr′vé	Mä loụin′	pär′lia ment	rī′val ry
Hōgue	măn′i fest	pa thĕt′ic	row′elṣ
hŏm′aġe	Märl′bȯr ȯ	Pa trō′clus	Rụ′nic
	Mär′mi on	pĕaṣ′ant	
in cär′nat ed	Mär′ner	pe cul′iar	St. Mä′lo
in dĭs′pu ta ble	mär′quis	pĕn′al ty	Scrĭp′tụreṣ
in sĕp′a ra ble	mär′veled	pen′çil ing	scrụ′pu lous
in ter rŏg′a- to ry	mā′tron	Pē′ter kin	sĕn si bĭl′i ty
	me lō′di ous	Phĭl ȧ dĕl′- phĭȧ	shȧ green′
in ter spẽrsed′	mĕn′aç ing		Shăn′non
Ire′land	Mẽr′çed	Pĭt′cairn	sĭ ĕr′ rȧ
irk′sȯme	Mĭd′i an	Plā′to	Sī′las

Sĭm'e on	tam böur ïne'	u năn'i mous	Wāke'field
sĭn̲'gu lar ly	Tan tăl'lon		wĕl'kin
sleīghts	tĕp'id	vā'grant	Wil hel mīne'
Sŏc'rȧ tĕs̩	thȳme	Van Brŭm'mel	Wĭn̲'kel rïēd
Sŏl'i dor	Tour vïlle'	Vĕd'der	Wō'burn
splĕn' e tic	trĕm'u lous	vĕn'er a ble	
spon tā'ne ous	tri bū'nal	vĕn'ġeançe	yeō'man ry
Stĭk'een	tûr'bū len çў	vĭc'ar	
sŭl'phur ous	Tўr'ol	vo lū'mi-	
Sўn'dic		nous ly	

NOTES—BIOGRAPHICAL AND EXPLANATORY

Page 9. Books. This selection is adapted from "Sesame and Lilies," a volume of essays addressed to girls, which Mr. Ruskin published in 1864. John Ruskin was an eminent English art critic and author (1819-1900). His writings are noted for the strength and purity of their style.

14. My Brute Neighbors. Henry David Thoreau (thō′rō), the author of "Walden" and other pleasing books on out-door subjects, was born at Concord, Massachusetts, 1817; died there, 1862. — *duellum*: a duel, a fight between two. — *bellum*: war, a fight among many. *Myrmidons*: a reference to the warriors of Achilles, who were said to have been originally ants.

21. September Days. *cicala* (chĕ kä′là) : an insect commonly called locust, or cicada. George Arnold was an American poet and journalist, born at New York, 1834; died, 1865.

22. Autumn's Mirth. Samuel Minturn Peck, an American poet, was born at Tuskaloosa, Alabama, 1854.

23. Under the Greenwood Tree. This little song is from Shakespeare's comedy, "As You Like It." — William Shakespeare, the greatest of English poets, was born at Stratford-on-Avon, 1654; died, 1616.

24. The High Court of Inquiry. Josiah Gilbert Holland, an American author, was born in Massachusetts, 1819; died in New York, 1881. He was the first editor of "The Century Magazine," and the writer of several excellent books, both prose and poetry. "Arthur Bonnicastle," his best novel, is supposed to be partly an autobiography.

31. Moses goes to the Fair. This extract is from "The Vicar of Wakefield," one of the most famous of English prose tales, published in 1766. The author, Oliver Goldsmith, was born at Pallas, Ireland, 1728; died at London, 1774. — *shagreen*: a kind of untanned leather.

36. A Legend of Bregenz. Adelaide Procter, an English poet, was born at London, 1825; died, 1864.

43. Parables. — The first of these parables, although usually attributed to Franklin, is of much earlier origin. It has been traced to

Jeremy Taylor, a famous English divine of the seventeenth century, who probably obtained it from a still older source.

51. The Man without a Country. The story was originally published in 1861, just at the beginning of the Civil War. Edward Everett Hale, a Unitarian clergyman, and the writer of many helpful books, was born at Boston, 1822.

63. The Battle of Lexington. George Bancroft, a famous American historian and statesman, was born at Worcester, Massachusetts, 1800; died, 1891. — *Louisburg*, a fortress on the coast of Cape Breton, captured from the French by New England soldiers in 1745.

69. The Bell of Liberty. Joel T. Headley, a once popular American writer, was born in New York, 1813; died, 1897.

73. The Rising in 1776. Thomas Buchanan Read, an American poet and painter, born in Pennsylvania, 1822; died, 1872. This selection is an extract from "The Wagoner of the Alleghanies," published in 1862.

77. Raleigh and Queen Elizabeth. This is a selection from the historical novel entitled "Kenilworth." Sir Walter Scott, a famous poet and novelist, was born at Edinburgh, Scotland, in 1771; died, 1832. — *liegeman:* a subject of a sovereign or lord.

83. Silas Marner and Eppie. George Eliot (Marian Evans), one of the greatest of English novelists, was born in Warwickshire, England, 1819; died, 1880.

93. The Bell of Atri. This is an old story put into rhyme. — *Syndic:* a chief magistrate. — *bryony* (sometimes spelled, briony): a climbing vine resembling the cucumber. — *Domeneddio:* equivalent in English to "Lord, God."

101. The Mocking Bird. Alexander Wilson (1776–1813) was a Scottish-American naturalist.

102. The Water Ouzel. *Water ouzel* (or ousel): sometimes called the American dipper, a bird found among the mountains and along the rivers of the West. — *sierra:* a ridge of mountains. — *cañon* (căn′yon): a narrow and very deep valley.

107. The Daffodils. William Wordsworth (1770–1850), a famous English poet, was the author of many pleasing short poems relating to nature or to domestic subjects.

120. The Sea Voyage. Charles Lamb (1775–1834) was one of the most pleasing of English essayists. His best works are in the volume entitled "Essays of Elia."

129. Oliver Goldsmith. This extract is from an essay by William Makepeace Thackeray, one of the most famous of English novelists (1811–1863). See note above referring to page 31.

153. The American Flag. This famous patriotic lyric, written in 1819, is the only poem that preserves the memory of its author, Joseph Rodman Drake, a once popular American writer (1795–1820).

161. The Lost Child. Henry Kingsley (1830–1876) was an English novelist and journalist. This selection is an extract from the novel entitled "Recollections of Geoffrey Hamlyn" (1859). — *pixies:* fairies.

170. Hervé Riel. *Hogue:* a cape on the coast of Holland. The battle here referred to occurred May 19, 1692. — *St. Malo:* a town on an island at the mouth of the Rance River, on the coast of France. — *Tourville:* a French admiral (1642–1701). — *Croisickese:* an inhabitant of Croisic, a fishing village at the mouth of the Loire. — *Grève:* the sandy shallows about the harbor of St. Malo. — *Damfreville* (D'Amfreville): a brave French officer who distinguished himself in the battle of La Hogue. — *Robert Browning:* a famous English poet (1812–1889).

189. The Battle of Blenheim. Blenheim is a village in Bavaria where the allied English, Germans, and Danes defeated the French in a great battle, August 13, 1704. Robert Southey (1774–1843) was a popular English poet and prose writer.

192. Burial of Sir John Moore. Sir John Moore, a British general, was killed in battle at Corunna, Spain, January 16, 1809. — Charles Wolfe, an Irish clergyman (1791–1823), is remembered only as the author of this very popular poem.

210. The Bells. Edgar Allan Poe, one of the most gifted of American poets, was born at Boston, 1809; died at Baltimore, 1849.

213. Little Gavroche. This selection is an extract translated from "Les Misérables," a famous French romance by Victor Hugo (1802–1885).

233. Speech and Silence. Thomas Carlyle, a celebrated essayist and historian, was born in Scotland, 1795; died at London, England, 1881.

THE GATEWAY SERIES
HENRY VAN DYKE, General Editor

SHAKESPEARE'S MERCHANT OF VENICE. Felix E. Schelling, University of Pennsylvania. $0.35.

SHAKESPEARE'S JULIUS CAESAR. Hamilton W. Mabie, "The Outlook." $0.35.

SHAKESPEARE'S MACBETH. T. M. Parrott, Princeton University. $0.40.

MILTON'S MINOR POEMS. M. A. Jordan, Smith College. $0.35.

ADDISON'S SIR ROGER DE COVERLEY PAPERS. C. T. Winchester, Wesleyan University. $0.40.

GOLDSMITH'S VICAR OF WAKEFIELD. James A. Tufts, Phillips Exeter Academy. $0.45.

BURKE'S SPEECH ON CONCILIATION. William MacDonald, Brown University. $0.35.

COLERIDGE'S ANCIENT MARINER. George E. Woodberry, Columbia University. $0.30.

SCOTT'S IVANHOE. Francis H. Stoddard, New York University, $0.50.

SCOTT'S LADY OF THE LAKE. R. M. Alden, Leland Stanford Jr. University. $0.40.

MACAULAY'S MILTON. Rev. E. L. Gulick, Lawrenceville School. $0.35.

MACAULAY'S ADDISON. Charles F. McClumpha, University of Minnesota. $0.35.

MACAULAY'S ADDISON AND JOHNSON. In one volume (McClumpha and Clark). $0.45.

MACAULAY'S LIFE OF JOHNSON. J. S. Clark, Northwestern University. $0.35.

CARLYLE'S ESSAY ON BURNS. Edwin Mims, Trinity College, North Carolina. $0.35.

GEORGE ELIOT'S SILAS MARNER. W. L. Cross, Yale University. $0.40.

TENNYSON'S PRINCESS. K. L. Bates, Wellesley College. $0.40.

TENNYSON'S GARETH AND LYNETTE, LANCELOT AND ELAINE, and THE PASSING OF ARTHUR. Henry van Dyke, Princeton University. $0.35.

EMERSON'S ESSAYS. Henry van Dyke, Princeton University. $0.35.

FRANKLIN'S AUTOBIOGRAPHY. Albert Henry Smyth, Central High School, Philadelphia.

GASKELL'S CRANFORD. Charles E. Rhodes, Lafayette High School, Buffalo. $0.40.

AMERICAN BOOK COMPANY

WEBSTER'S
SCHOOL DICTIONARIES
Revised Editions

THESE Dictionaries have been thoroughly revised, entirely reset, and made to conform to that great standard authority—Webster's International Dictionary.

WEBSTER'S PRIMARY SCHOOL DICTIONARY $0.48
   Containing over 20,000 words and meanings, with over 400 illustrations.

WEBSTER'S COMMON SCHOOL DICTIONARY $0.72
   Containing over 25,000 words and meanings, with over 500 illustrations.

WEBSTER'S HIGH SCHOOL DICTIONARY, $0.98
   Containing about 37,000 words and definitions, and an appendix giving a pronouncing vocabulary of Biblical, Classical, Mythological, Historical, and Geographical proper names, with over 800 illustrations.

WEBSTER'S ACADEMIC DICTIONARY
   Cloth, $1.50; Indexed $1.80
   Half Calf, $2.75; Indexed 3.00
   Abridged directly from the International Dictionary, and giving the orthography, pronunciations, definitions, and synonyms of about 60,000 words in common use, with an appendix containing various useful tables, with over 800 illustrations.

SPECIAL EDITIONS
   Webster's Countinghouse Dictionary. Sheep,
      Indexed $2.40
   Webster's Handy Dictionary 15
   Webster's Pocket Dictionary 57
      The same. Roan, Flexible 69
      The same. Roan, Tucks 78
      The same. Morocco, Indexed 90

AMERICAN BOOK COMPANY

RODDY'S GEOGRAPHIES

By JUSTIN RODDY, M.S., Department of Geography, First Pennsylvania State Normal School, Millersville, Pa.

| Elementary Geography . $0.50 | Complete Geography . . $1.00 |

THIS "information" series meets a distinct demand for new geographies which are thoroughly up to date, and adapted for general use, rather than for a particular use in a highly specialized and organized ideal system. While not too technical and scientific, it includes sufficient physiographic information for the needs of most teachers.

¶ An adequate amount of material is included in each book to meet the requirements of those grades for which it is designed. This matter is presented so simply that the pupil can readily understand it, and so logically that it can easily be taught by the average teacher.

¶ The simplicity of the older methods of teaching this subject is combined with just so much of the modern scientific methods of presentation as is thoroughly adapted to elementary grades. Only enough physiography is included to develop the fundamental relations of geography, and to animate and freshen the study, without overloading it in this direction.

¶ The physical maps of the grand divisions are drawn to the same scale, thus enabling the pupil to form correct concepts of the relative size of countries. The political and more detailed maps are not mere skeletons, giving only the names which are required by the text, but are full enough to serve all ordinary purposes for reference. In addition, they show the principal railroads and canals, the head of navigation on all important rivers, and the standard divisions of time.

¶ The illustrations are new and fresh, reproduced mostly from photographs collected from all parts of the world. Formal map studies or questions accompany each map, directing attention to the most important features.

AMERICAN BOOK COMPANY

NEW ROLFE SHAKESPEARE
Edited by WILLIAM J. ROLFE, Litt.D.
40 volumes, each, $0.56

THE popularity of Rolfe's Shakespeare has been extraordinary. Since its first publication in 1870-83 it has been used more widely, both in schools and colleges, and by the general reading public, than any similar edition ever issued. It is to-day the standard annotated edition of Shakespeare for educational purposes.

¶ As teacher and lecturer Dr. Rolfe has been constantly in touch with the recent notable advances made in Shakespearian investigation and criticism; and this revised edition he has carefully adjusted to present conditions.

¶ The introductions and appendices have been entirely rewritten, and now contain the history of the plays and poems; an account of the sources of the plots, with copious extracts from the chronicles and novels from which the poet drew his material; and general comments by the editor, with selections from the best English and foreign criticism.

¶ The notes are very full, and include all the historical, critical, and illustrative material needed by the teacher, as well as by the student, and general reader. Special features in the notes are the extent to which Shakespeare is made to explain himself by parallel passages from his works; the frequent Bible illustrations; the full explanations of allusions to the manners and customs of the period; and descriptions of the localities connected with the poet's life and works. Attention is given to Shakespeare's grammar and metre, and to textual variations when these are of unusual importance and interest.

¶ New notes have also been substituted for those referring to other volumes of the edition, so that each volume is now absolutely complete in itself. The pictorial illustrations are all new, those retained from the old edition being re-engraved. The form of the books has also been modified, the page being made smaller to adjust them to pocket use.

AMERICAN BOOK COMPANY

CHOICE LITERATURE

By SHERMAN WILLIAMS, Ph.D., New York State Institute Conductor

Book One, for Primary Grades	$0.22
Book Two, for Primary Grades	.25
Book One, for Intermediate Grades	.28
Book Two, for Intermediate Grades	.35
Book One, for Grammar Grades	.40
Book Two, for Grammar Grades	.50

ALTHOUGH these books can be used to excellent advantage in teaching children how to read, the main purpose of the series is to teach them what to read; to create and foster a taste for good literature. The selections are carefully made and graded.

¶ The books for the primary grades include selections from the Mother Goose Melodies, nursery classics, fairy stories from Hans Christian Andersen, and the Grimm brothers, Æsop's Fables, memory gems, children's poems by such writers as Stevenson, Alice Cary, Tennyson, Lydia Maria Child, Cecilia Thaxter, and a few prose selections among which Ruskin's King of the Golden River is given complete.

¶ In the books for intermediate grades the reading matter is more advanced. Here are given such delightful selections as Aladdin, Pandora, The Sunken Treasure, Wonder Book, Tanglewood Tales, Rip Van Winkle, The Barefoot Boy, A Visit from St. Nicholas, Children in the Wood, The Last of the Mohicans, Tom Brown's School Days, etc.

¶ The volumes for the grammar grades are made up of the best English and American literature. Among the eminent writers represented are Scott, Dickens, George Eliot, Irving, Addison, Patrick Henry, Lamb, Lincoln, Webster, Bryant, Burns, Goldsmith, Tennyson, Newman, Poe, Shakespeare, Coleridge, Gray, Macaulay, Holmes, Longfellow, Lowell, Milton, Whittier, and Byron.

AMERICAN BOOK COMPANY

GRADED WORK IN ARITHMETIC

By S. W. BAIRD, Principal, Franklin Grammar School, Wilkesbarre, Pa.

First Year	Boards, $0.18	Cloth,	$0.20
Second Year	" .18	"	.20
Third Year	" .20	"	.25
Fourth Year	" .20	"	.25
Fifth Year	" .20	"	.25
Sixth Year		"	.25
Seventh Year		"	.25
Eighth Year		"	.25
Practical Arithmetic for Grammar Grades		"	.65

THIS series consists of eight books designed for use in all the grades of elementary schools. It furnishes to pupils text-books carefully planned to strengthen their powers of mathematical reasoning, at the same time presenting a range of topics sufficiently comprehensive to familiarize them with the important practical applications of the science to the wants of common life. The Practical Arithmetic, with the first four books, forms a five-book series.

¶ The books abound in combinations of oral and written work, and in copious examples for drills and reviews. Each subject is treated both pedagogically and mathematically. Common sense and the keen logic of the mathematician are shown on every page. Each book begins with a review of the essential principles studied in the previous book. The subjects are taken up alternately, in accordance with the ability of the child, and not as complete wholes.

¶ Great care has been taken in the selection of illustrative examples and operations. Explanations and analyses have been given in full, in order that the principles involved may be easily and clearly understood by the pupil.

AMERICAN BOOK COMPANY

UNITED STATES HISTORIES

By JOHN BACH McMASTER, Professor of American History, University of Pennsylvania

Primary History, $0.60   School History, $1.00   Brief History, $1.00

THESE standard histories are remarkable for their freshness and vigor, their authoritative statements, and their impartial treatment. They give a well-proportioned and interesting narrative of the chief events in our history, and are not loaded down with extended and unnecessary bibliographies. The illustrations are historically authentic, and show, besides well-known scenes and incidents, the implements and dress characteristic of the various periods. The maps are clear and full, and well executed.

¶ The PRIMARY HISTORY is simply and interestingly written, with no long or involved sentences. Although brief, it touches upon all matters of real importance to schools in the founding and building of our country, but copies beyond the understanding of children are omitted. The summaries at the end of the chapters, besides serving to emphasize the chief events, are valuable for review.

¶ In the SCHOOL HISTORY by far the larger part of the book has been devoted to the history of the United States since 1783. From the beginning the attention of the student is directed to causes and results rather than to isolated events. Special prominence is given to the social and economic development of the country.

¶ In the BRIEF HISTORY nearly one-half the book is devoted to the colonial period. The text proper, while brief, is complete in itself; and footnotes in smaller type permit of a more comprehensive course if desired. Short summaries, and suggestions for collateral reading, are provided.

AMERICAN BOOK COMPANY

CARPENTER'S READERS
By FRANK G. CARPENTER

GEOGRAPHICAL READERS

North America	. $0.60	Africa	$0.60
South America	. .60	Australia, Our Colonies,	
Europe . . .	. .70	and Other Islands of the	
Asia	. .60	Sea	.60

READERS ON COMMERCE AND INDUSTRY

How the World is Fed . $0.60 | How the World is Clothed $0.60

CARPENTER'S Geographical Readers supplement the regular text-books on the subject, giving life and interest to the study. They are intensely absorbing, being written by the author on the spots described, and presenting an accurate pen-picture of places and peoples. The style is simple and easy, and throughout each volume there runs a strong personal note which makes the reader feel that he is actually seeing everything with his own eyes.

¶ The books give a good idea of the various peoples, their strange customs and ways of living, and to some extent of their economic condition. At the same time, there is included a graphic description of the curious animals, rare birds, wonderful physical features, natural resources, and great industries of each country. The illustrations for the most part are reproductions of photographs taken by the author. The maps show the route taken over each continent.

¶ The Readers on Commerce and Industry give a personal and living knowledge of the great world of commerce and industry. The children visit the great food centers and see for themselves how the chief food staples are produced and prepared for use, and they travel in the same way over the globe investigating the sources of their clothing. The journeys are along geographical lines, and while studying the industries the children are learning about localities, trade routes, and the other features of transportation and commerce.

AMERICAN BOOK COMPANY

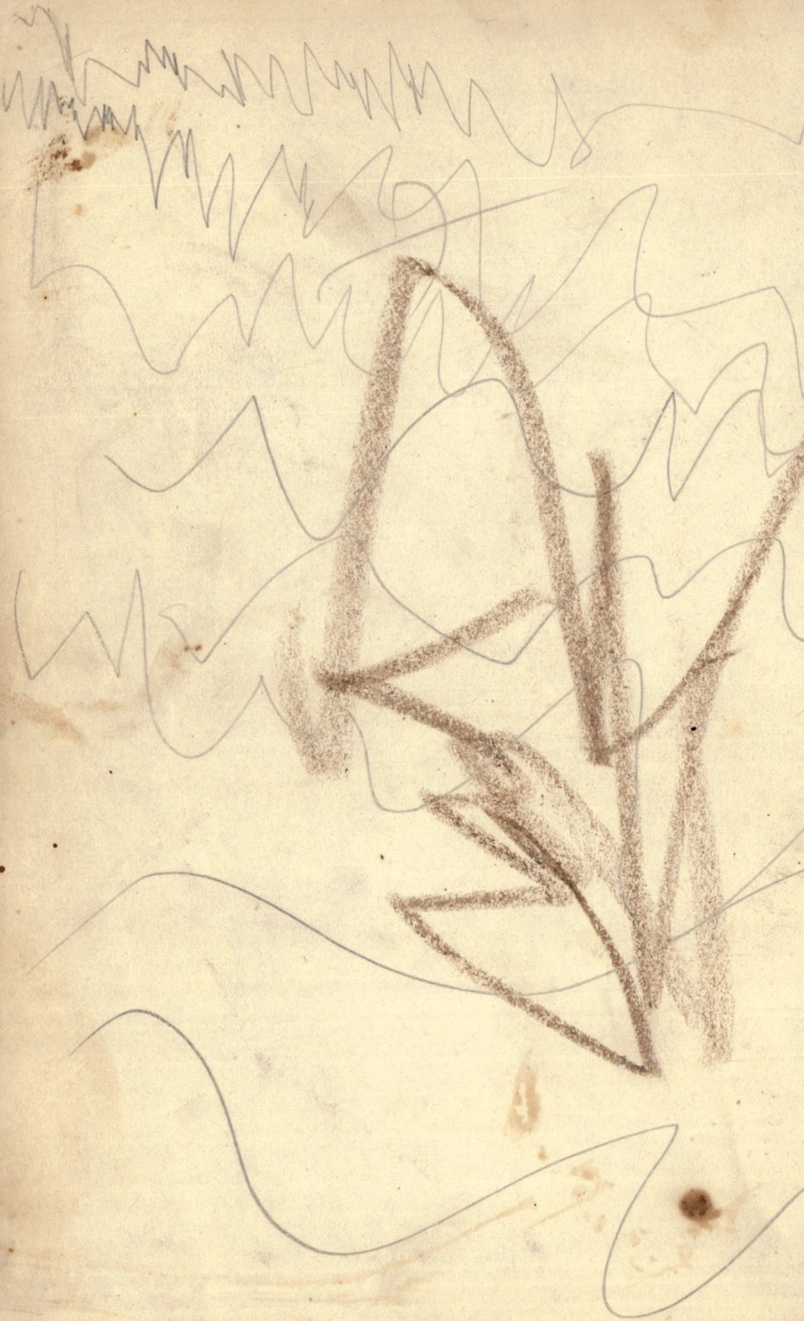